HOME

COCKTAIL

BIBLE

Hardie Grant

QUADRILLE

Publishing Director: Sarah Lavelle

Recipe Developer: Seb Munsch

Copy Editor: Euan Ferguson

Art Direction: Claire Rochford

Designer: Alicia House

Photographer: Matt Russell

Drink Stylist: Loïc Parisot

Prop Stylist: Max Robinson

Head of Production: Stephen Lang

Senior Production Controller: Nikolaus Ginelli

First published in 2021 by Quadrille,
an imprint of Hardie Grant Publishing

Quadrille
52–54 Southwark Street
London SE1 1UN
quadrille.com

Cataloguing in Publication Data: a catalogue record
for this book is available from the British Library.

978 1 78713 805 6

Printed in China

MIX
Paper from
responsible sources
FSC™ C020056

CONTENTS

INTRODUCTION

Get ready to mix things up!

Truly great cocktails should be simple to make, look fabulous and taste extraordinary. Perfect every time and with minimum fuss, these recipes are designed to make every moment feel magical.

Cocktails instantly invoke a sense of occasion. Formal, relaxed, celebratory, era-evoking, mood-provoking or calmly reflective, these clever combinations are your fast-track to a world of liquid treats.

The recipes in this book are as varied as Elton John's wardrobe – and just as imaginative! Alongside the classics, brand-new ideas are ready to entertain you and your guests with the way they look and taste. They're sweet or sharp, spicy or scented; they can be creamy, sparkling or pure and invigorating as a mountain brook. Your preference should always take the lead in picking the perfect drink. On a hot day, quenching is key; in the frosts of winter something a little more comforting is called for. And, most importantly, what bottles have you got to hand?

One insight that never changes is the spirit of the cocktail. From the juniper jolt of gin to the warmth of whisky, this book is divided by headline bottles to build a range of flavours from the base drink up.

The simplest decision of which spirit you're in the mood for will always guide you to the right cocktail. And, of course, how inventive you're feeling will inform whether you want to keep things quick and simple or try something a little more adventurous.

The history of cocktails has a lexicon of intrigue stretching back more than a hundred years. Both classics and new recipes respect the heritage and evolution of mixing drinks. The Mint Julep, for example, is iconic – such brilliant balance from a few simple ingredients. That principle guides every recipe in this book, which also follows my rule that cocktails should be convenient as well as classy. Setting jargon aside in favour of practical facts, my flavour wheels offer instant inspiration for which flavours work best with each spirit, so you can have a go at creating your own cocktails too. There are 200 recipes to choose from, but the method for each is succinct and I've offered tips and variations for you to have fun with while you're making the cocktail as well as sipping it.

Bringing the wow factor to your fingertips with simple core ingredients, my Capsule Cocktail Cabinet contains all the essential mixers, spirits, bitters and syrups you'll ever need to take your creativity to the next level. As for kit, you don't need much to achieve the results of a seasoned pro. In a few short steps and with simple skills, your cocktails will be enviable, divine and irresistible to all.

Celebrations, like the greatest adventures, begin with small ideas. Let this book be the springboard to smashing times at home, with your cocktail creations flowing like the best conversation. With these recipes under your belt, you're only ever a few moments from stratospheric levels of enjoyment.

Time to take your taste buds into orbit!

CAPSULE COCKTAIL CABINET

Vodka

Rum

Tequila

Gin

Brandy

Simple syrup

Sparkling wine

White wine

Red wine

Dry vermouth

Sweet vermouth

Campari

Triple sec or Cointreau

Apricot brandy

Peach schnapps

Blue curaçao

Orange curaçao

Crème de cassis

Grenadine

St-Germain elderflower liqueur

Amaretto hazelnut liqueur

Kahlua coffee liqueur

Baileys Irish Cream

Crème de menthe

Angostura Bitters

KIT

Shaker
A shaker is the single most useful piece of equipment for cocktail making – if you can find an insulated one, so much the better for keeping those cocktails icy-cold.

Strainer
This is a mini-sieve that will filter out bits of fruit or ice to achieve an ultra-smooth texture.

Long bar spoon
A long-handled bar spoon enables you to get to the very bottom of a shaker or tall glass to stir up the contents.

Peeler
By far the easiest way to make those impressive strips of lemon and orange that top the perfect cocktail is with an ordinary potato peeler. No knife or chopping board necessary!

Squeezer
This is useful but not strictly necessary – it's handy for fresh limes and lemons, but you can always use your hands and a firm squeeze!

Muddler
This is like a pestle, usually made of wood, and used to bash up spices or tenderise fruit. You could use the end of a rolling pin (with care!).

Corkscrew
Everyone has their own emergency method for getting into a bottle of beer or wine when on a picnic with no corkscrew, but let's face it, it's jolly handy.

GLASSWARE

Wine glass
Don't rush out and buy any new wine glasses for cocktails – you'll want something with a large bowl as most cocktails served in wine glasses will probably also feature ice (such as spritzes), and perhaps fruit and herbs, so the glass needs to be roomy.

Hurricane
These can vary in shape, but a hurricane is usually a tall tumbler with a low bowl and a flared rim, used for serving mixed and fruity drinks including a Singapore Sling or a Piña Colada.

Rocks
A rocks glass is a stocky, chunky tumbler, most recognisable as the classic whisky glass. A standard tumbler is medium-height and flat-based, and can be either straight-sided, flared or curved.

Shot
A shot glass or shooter traditionally contains a single measure of spirit, but since single or measured quantities vary according to where in the world you live, there is no standard size of glass. To make the shot-based cocktails in this book you'll want enough volume to contain a couple of measures.

Collins
This is usually a straight-sided, tall tumbler with enough volume and height to contain lots of ice.

Coupe
The traditional coupe shape is the classic stemmed 'belle époque' Champagne glass, since replaced in popularity by the taller flute. 'Coupe' means 'cup', and it's that curved, elegant shape that's so visually appealing when you serve a cocktail.

Martini
The martini glass is the quintessential cocktail glass – stemmed, with a triangular, straight-edged bowl, it's perfect for so many types of drinks and you'll definitely be needing one or two. Or three, or four...

Flute
Elegant flute glasses come in many subtly different shapes – they need to be tall and thin to prevent all those beautiful bubbles escaping.

Speciality
Occasionally a drink calls for a glass with a handle, usually because it's a hot punch or a frosty beverage like a Mint Julep. And sometimes you'll want a tall pitcher of a batch cocktail, to refrigerate and pour at your leisure.

GARNISHES

Fruit
A twist, peel or slice of a fruit like lemon, orange or lime can make all the difference – that final spritz of citrus oil that brings the cocktail together. If you like, you can flash with a blowtorch – or just give your peel a little squeeze as you drop it into the drink.

Maraschino cherries
Ah, the glorious maraschino cherry, a vital component of cocktails like the Manhattan; maraschino liqueur itself is an essential in so many drinks. Pop them onto a cocktail stick, or in the bottom of a martini glass for a sweet treat when you get to the bottom. Slurp!

Olives
Essential for the savoury rush of the famous Dirty Martini, small green olives are for the cocktail connoisseur – they need to be stone-in for authenticity and maximum flavour.

Cocktail onions and pickles
We're into serious savoury territory here – a Gibson would just be a Martini without an onion, and a pickle on the side of your Bloody Mary will make it a super-sensation of sweet, sour, salty and savoury.

Salt
Not just for a Margarita, creating an impressive salt rim is easy as pie – cover a small plate with salt, take a wedge of fruit (usually lime) and rub it around the edge of your glass. Place it upturned in the salt and, hey presto.

Herb sprigs and dried flowers
Herbs and flowers make a wonderfully aromatic and attractive garnish – you'll be familiar with mint in a Mojito but basil, thyme and rosemary are also magical ingredients. Use the softest leaves from the tip of the stalk. Dried rose petals look striking scattered over a drink, too.

 Fruit

 Herbal

 Floral

 Savoury

 Misc

SYRUPS

Simple Syrup

You can buy simple syrup (sugar syrup) as well as a huge range of flavoured syrups, but they're also very easy to make at home. Simple syrup uses a basic 1:1 ratio.

150g or ¾ cup caster (superfine) sugar

150ml or ¾ cup water

Equipment: Pan, spoon, funnel, glass bottle

Add the ingredients to a pan and stir well

Heat gently to a simmer (do not boil)

Keep stirring until the sugar has fully dissolved

Remove from the heat

Leave to cool before using a funnel to pour the mixture into a clean glass bottle

You can store the syrup in the fridge for up to a month

For herb syrups, add a small handful of herbs to the mixture as you're heating it so the flavours can infuse. Strain through a sieve before decanting into a bottle.

For cinnamon syrup, add a cinnamon stick to the mixture as you're heating. Leave to cool and infuse before straining.

For vanilla syrup, add a vanilla pod to the mixture. Leave to cool and infuse before straining.

For rose syrup, add 1 tbsp rose water to the mixture.

To make honey syrup use a 2:1 ratio: i.e. 100g or 6 tbsp honey to 50ml or 3 tbsp water.

For honey ginger syrup, add 1 tbsp crystallized ginger to the syrup as you're heating. Strain before using.

Wine Syrups

Like simple syrup, wine syrups use a basic 1:1 ratio.

100g or ½ cup caster (superfine) sugar

100ml or ½ cup wine

Equipment: Pan, spoon, funnel, glass bottle

Add the ingredients to a pan and stir well

Heat gently to a simmer (do not boil)

Keep stirring until the sugar has fully dissolved

Remove from the heat

Leave to cool before using a funnel to pour the mixture into a clean glass bottle

You can store the syrup in the fridge for up to a month

Wine syrups add roundness and depth of flavour to cocktails. It's definitely worth experimenting by adding a dash to your favourite cocktails.

Red The structure of red wine is what really adds to the depth of flavour. It goes well with darker spirits. Avoid anything too aged and stick to good-value, mellow types such as Rioja joven from Spain, shiraz from Australia or merlot from Chile.

Rosé A nice addition to tequila and gin-based drinks. Has the bonus of turning clear drinks blush pink.

White Go for unoaked. Sauvignon blanc is a good option, or stick to Italian whites for a safe bet. White wine syrup blends particularly well with gin-based cocktails.

VODKA

Vodka is as elusive and captivating as a melting snowball. It's often distilled from grains, sugar beet or potatoes, but in fact you can make vodka from pretty much anything, depending on what grows well where you are. Potato vodka is creamy and lush, grape vodka tends to be zingy, wheat brings freshness, corn has a sweet tinge and barley a nutty twist. Finding your favourite is key – don't be afraid to taste them neat and deploy them liberally in these cocktails. I personally rate Chase vodka from the UK, which is made from their own base potato spirit and works a charm in all cocktails from Martinis to Mudslides. Purity is what counts here – since it's clear as a mountain brook it allows you to build and blend colour as well as flavour your cocktails beautifully. And each vodka carries a distinctive taste and texture, so whether your vodka comes from Russia, Poland or anywhere in the world, it brings character to your cocktail.

And, of course, flavoured vodkas introduce a whole new stratum of splendour. While I was a student living in Edinburgh in the 1990s, Bar Kohl (unfortunately now closed, was on George IV Bridge) taught me so much about flavoured vodkas. The bar created its own, and while some were sweet and others exotic, I always fell for the fiery chilli concoctions, which lit up my life. Flavouring vodkas stretches back through the centuries; herbs and spices pep up the spirit and you can easily make your own. Citrus is my preferred route – always unwaxed. Use the peel rather than the fruit, cut into fine strips carefully avoiding pith, then infuse in your vodka. It takes around three days – you don't need that much, one or two lemons or oranges will be plenty for a litre (4 cups), and you can add a bit of sugar if you like. You can also mix different citrus peels if you fancy creating your own concoction. Give it a shake if you're passing the bottle, and once it's done, strain off the fruit and start making cracking cocktails.

When you're selecting your favourite vodka, it pays to compare and contrast a few side by side. You may think you have a favourite brand, but tasting it back-to-back with other bottles often produces a fresh result – you'll be surprised! Alongside the flavour and texture, watch for how long the flavours linger. Similar to wine, a great vodka will be persistent. And as long as you love the taste, here's hoping it'll last forever!

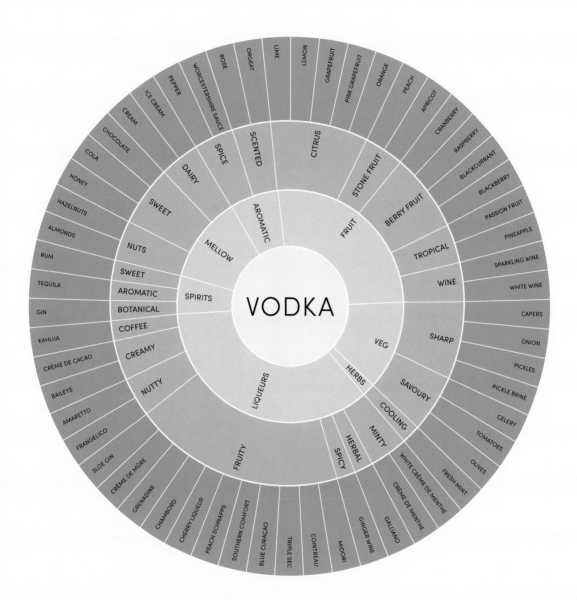

DRY VODKA MARTINI

Famously James Bond's favourite drink, but when I used to dine with him, Roger Moore would always insist he preferred a Gin Martini. In this case, indulging in 007's tipple of choice is taken to the next level by that discreet whisper of orange bitters, which for me works best with a twist. Go with your garnish here – if you're in the mood for salty, hit the dirty button and unleash the olives.

The Perfect Martini is highly underrated and offers a pathway of indulgence where fruity and zingy flavours unite on a bridge to the Excellence Isles. Be warned, one always leads to two, and rather like the Excellence Isles (I made them up), no one really knows how many there ultimately are. You'll notice I prefer to stir rather than shake my Martini. Up to you – the only reason for me is that I find it dilutes the drink less, and avoids chips of ice or cloudiness. I want my Martini to be as light and pure as the stratosphere through which it propels me on the very first sip. As I like to say, cruising altitude without the need for take-off. The immediacy of the Vodka Martini means you're already off duty as soon as you start thinking about making one. Like now.

75ml (2½oz) vodka

15ml (½oz) dry vermouth (traditionally Noilly Prat)

Dash orange bitters (optional)

Ice: Cubed

Garnish: Any one of olive, lemon twist, lemon zest, cocktail onion, caperberry

Equipment: Cocktail shaker, long bar spoon, strainer

Fill a shaker with ice

Add all the ingredients

Stir well to chill

Strain into a chilled glass

Add your preferred garnish

The colder the ingredients the better, so keep your base spirit in the freezer before making if you can. There are a huge number of different Martinis but the classics are **Dry**, **Sweet** or **Perfect**.

There are many ratio variations – experiment until you find the one you like.

For a **Sweet Martini** replace dry vermouth for sweet vermouth.

For a **Perfect Martini** use equal parts dry and sweet vermouth.

For a **Dirty Martini** add a dash of olive brine or olive bitters.

COSMOPOLITAN

To me, the Cosmopolitan is *Sex in the City*. Everyone was drinking them in the 90s thanks to the hit TV show and while all good cocktails peak and plummet in popularity, the Cosmo endures as a modern classic. Lemon vodka in this recipe adds raciness and dials up the sweet and sour thrills with each sip. The tension framed in the recipe is what makes this drink so special – it tastes instantly dynamic and also looks like the best night out in Manhattan.

45ml (1½oz) lemon vodka

15ml (½oz) Cointreau

15ml (½oz) freshly squeezed lime juice

30ml (1oz) cranberry juice

Ice: Cubed

Garnish: Orange twist

Equipment: Cocktail shaker, strainer

Fill a shaker with ice

Add all the ingredients

Shake vigorously to chill

Strain into a chilled glass

For a professional finish, flame the zest of an orange twist over the drink and drop in to garnish

BLACK RUSSIAN

Kahlua and vodka. It seems naughty and it is – full marks for bravery if you try this. The name comes from the deep colour of Kahlua and the Russian bit is a nod to vodka. Vodka is legendary, and the thing is, Kahlua is a more serious drink than you think – it brings sweet depth, leaving the lighter side of enlivening to the main spirit. The little caffeine jolt also makes this an excellent candidate to kick the party off (as well as extend it). The tale of the Black Russian begins in the 1940s with Perle Mesta, American Ambassador to Luxembourg, for whom this drink was said to be created – she was the human incarnation of the party spirit. And since 1936 when Kahlua was first concocted in Mexico, its legacy is a bottle so iconic that it defies fashion and trends. I love the stuff – you need more of it in your life.

45ml (1½oz) vodka

22.5ml (¾oz) Kahlua

Ice: Cubed

Equipment: Long bar spoon

Fill a glass with ice

Add all the ingredients

Stir gently to chill

An alternative to a Black Russian involves adding 22.5ml (¾oz) cola.

For a **White Russian** add 30ml (1oz) single (light) cream.

For a **Nutty Russian** add 22.5ml (¾oz) Frangelico to the Black Russian recipe (no cola).

COLORADO BULLDOG

Slick, sweet, rich and voluptuous. To me, this is the liquid version of skiing. Or at least that warm resonance that a day on the slopes brings, which I guess is quite similar to the afterglow of a vigorous dancefloor strut. I first started drinking these in the French Alps, my favourite place to slide idly down mountains. That must be why the mood takes me straight to après ski. There's a satin sparkle at play here that reminds me of light bouncing off snowy peaks and differentiates it from a White Russian. In my book that canoodling texture is just perfect for playing around the slopes of Mount Escapade.

37.5ml (1¼oz) vodka

22.5ml (¾oz) Kahlua

22.5ml (¾oz) single (light) cream

30ml (1oz) cola

Ice: Cubed

Equipment: Cocktail shaker, strainer

Fill a shaker with ice

Add all the ingredients except the cola

Shake vigorously to chill

Strain into a glass filled with ice

Float cola on top

MUDSLIDE

The Mudslide is my wife Sophie's secret
favourite. Her love affair with this cocktail
erupted in Mexico at the swim-up bar in the
Grand Velas Riviera Maya resort. I'd landed
a job writing a travel piece for the *Mail on
Sunday* and together with my family had
a magic time relaxing in the sunshine and
romping around Mayan ruins. Sophie found
the Mudslide to be the perfect partner for
languishing in the sunshine and after some
careful experimentation I concurred. This is
the ultimate boozy smoothie and while the
feeling of a sun-drenched poolside bar can
easily be evoked, the best thing about this
drink is the dreamy feeling of holiday that
the flavours exude. Book yourself a break
and mix one up right now.

22.5ml (¾oz) vodka

22.5ml (¾oz) Baileys

22.5ml (¾oz) Kahlua

2 scoops vanilla ice cream

Ice: Crushed

Garnish: Chocolate sauce drizzle

Equipment: Blender

Add a small handful of crushed ice to
a blender cup

Add all the ingredients

Blend until smooth

Drizzle chocolate sauce around the inside
of your glass

Pour over the blended drink

Drizzle more chocolate sauce on top

For a non-blended version, omit the ice cream
and crushed ice. Shake the ingredients with
cubed ice and add 60ml (2oz) single (light) cream.
Serve over ice.

SLOW COMFORTABLE SCREW

Brunch! This is my favourite for a brunchtime treat and it builds on the Screwdriver's fruity balanced zing. The rapid practicality of the Screwdriver is said to come from American engineers working in Iran, who mixed their drinks with handy tools. This cocktail gets a little more finessing from the float of sloe gin, which is what brings the sense of occasion. My most memorable Slow Comfortable Screw was late morning in Miami, right on the shore – it set me up for an all-day feeling of magic hour.

37.5ml (1¼oz) vodka

15ml (½oz) Southern Comfort

90ml (3oz) freshly squeezed orange juice

15ml (½oz) sloe gin

Ice: Cubed

Garnish: Orange slice

Equipment: Long bar spoon

Fill a glass with ice

Add all the ingredients except the sloe gin

Stir gently to chill

Float the sloe gin on top of the drink

Garnish with an orange slice

There are many variations of a SCS.

Slow = sloe gin. Comfortable = Southern Comfort. Screw = the freshly squeezed orange juice from a Screwdriver.

Add Galliano and it's a **Slow Comfortable Screw Up Against the Wall** ('Wall' from Harvey Wallbanger).

Add amaretto and it's a **Slow Comfortable Screw With a Kiss**.

ESPRESSO MARTINI

EASY VARIATION

As quick, simple and rhythmical as Peter Gabriel's 'Sledgehammer'. One of those tracks that, if you play it loudly enough, always sounds better than you think it is. This recipe is the same: on paper it looks like a simple cheat of two parts coffee liqueur to one of espresso, yet when you pour it, the impact of that ratio is as awesome as the percussion's precision in 'Sledgehammer'. So quick to make and divine to share. Crank up the stereo or sip it on a bench and pretend you're in a stationary open-top car after lunch in Monte Carlo.

60ml (2oz) cold brew coffee liqueur

30ml (1oz) freshly brewed espresso

Ice: Cubed

Garnish: Coffee beans

Equipment: Cocktail shaker, strainer

Fill a shaker with ice

Add all the ingredients

Shake vigorously to chill

Strain into a chilled glass

Garnish with three coffee beans

ESPRESSO MARTINI

The three coffee beans used to garnish an Espresso Martini represent health, wealth and happiness. The little gap that grows when you remove them signifies extending the evening with enlivening conversation and deep reflection. Fair warning: Espresso Martinis may make your leg jiggle and you will sometimes find yourself irrepressibly enhanced on the dancefloor. Is it worth making the freshly brewed espresso? It sure is. That vivid flavour comes from no other source as splendid and enhances the nuanced layers of sumptuous coffee from the Kahlua. And while I'm not saying you should replace your morning cup of coffee with this drink, I will say that Espresso Martinis make a surprisingly splendid start to a day off. And (whisper it) they also rock as an alternative to a Bloody Mary the morning after a big night in.

45ml (1½oz) vodka

22.5ml (¾oz) Kahlua

30ml (1oz) freshly brewed espresso

7.5ml (¼oz) simple syrup (see page 11)

Ice: Cubed

Garnish: Coffee beans

Equipment: Cocktail shaker, strainer

Fill a shaker with ice

Add all the ingredients

Shake vigorously to chill

Strain into a chilled glass

Garnish with three coffee beans

MOSCOW MULE

Ah, this takes me back to my days living in Edinburgh, the city that taught me how to drink steadily and over a decent time frame. Drinks really shouldn't be hurried, and the Moscow Mule in 90s Auld Reekie (as Edinburgh is nicknamed) was the Mojito of its day. You could count on pretty much any bar to make you the best iteration imaginable. I remember sipping them in my heat rounds of the BBC's Young Comedian of the Year or some such contest. Yes, my stand-up days were short-lived and burned all the brighter thanks to the Moscow Mule. I seem to remember a particular routine I did about Clairol's Nice'n Easy hair colouring campaign going down particularly well. Never as well as the drink though. Spice, sweetness and aromatics got me through long, dutiful nights in crystal Scottish winters learning how to drink slowly and with great determination. A beast of burden it ain't, though. Its inception is said to be at the hands of two friends in LA in the 1940s, one who'd acquired the rights to Smirnoff vodka and the other who had a surplus of ginger beer on his hands. With more fortunate timing – a girlfriend who'd inherited a copper factory – vodka mixed with ginger beer served in a copper mug took the world by storm. And I was siphoned from a career in comedy into drinking professionally for a living. Win win.

45ml (1½oz) vodka

15ml (½oz) freshly squeezed lime juice

7.5ml (¼oz) simple syrup (see page 11)

90ml (3oz) fiery ginger beer, to top

Ice: Crushed

Garnish: Lime slice and mint sprig

Equipment: Long bar spoon

Fill a mug or glass two-thirds with crushed ice

Add all the ingredients except the ginger beer

Churn gently to chill

Top with ginger beer and cap with more crushed ice

Garnish with a lime slice and a sprig of mint

Swap out the vodka for tequila to make a **Mexican Mule**.

For a **Kentucky Mule** use bourbon.

Experiment with your favourite spirits to find a combination you like.

BLOODY MARY

Every morning is a suitable morning to experiment with the best iteration of a Bloody Mary, and this recipe is so good it presents the perfect excuse to mix and marvel. I am a fiend for sharp flavours and I once read somewhere that pickle brine is packed with electrolytes: true or not, it's a good enough reason for me to add that flash of invigoration to the drink. And as for spice, I like mine so fiery that Mount Etna would blush. Up to you. But the game changer here is fino or manzanilla sherry. Both are clear and bright and full of saline, with an almost green, olive-like punch. They deliver on texture, umami and zippy, upbeat balance. Think of it like adding springs to your heels before leaping over the silvery Moon. Surely all the exertion has earned you a sip of this liquid reboot?

45ml (1½oz) vodka

7.5ml (¼oz) fino or manzanilla (dry) sherry

7.5ml (¼oz) freshly squeezed lemon juice

7.5ml (¼oz) pickle brine

120ml (4oz) tomato juice

½ tsp celery salt

½ tsp black pepper

2 splashes each hot sauce and Worcestershire sauce, or to taste

Ice: Cubed

Garnish: Celery, lime wedge and pickle

Equipment: Long bar spoon

Fill a glass with ice

Add all the ingredients

Stir well to chill

Garnish with celery stick, lime wedge and a pickle

Tomato juice can be replaced with your favourite multi-vegetable juice, or use Clamato for a **Bloody Caesar**.

See Bloody Maria recipe (page 126) for a tequila alternative.

GREEN EYES

My friend Seb Munsch's passion for cocktails is unrivalled and he knows how much I love a green cocktail. Just ask him about the time I came up with the idea for the Disco Dancing Hulk! When it comes to crafting cocktails, among the greatest pearls of wisdom is that blue curaçao can turn any drink green – if you know how to use it. In this drink, it's the combination with orange juice that transforms blue to glowing green. And while the colour of the Green Eyes is fantastic, it's also a great cocktail to kick off an evening thanks to its equally striking flavour.

37.5ml (1¼oz) vodka

15ml (½oz) blue curaçao

90ml (3oz) freshly squeezed orange juice

Ice: Cubed

Garnish: Lime wedge

Equipment: Cocktail shaker, strainer

Fill a shaker with ice

Add all the ingredients

Shake vigorously to chill

Strain into a glass filled with ice

Garnish with a lime wedge

HARVEY WALLBANGER

How could this cocktail ever go out of fashion? It's a step up from the Screwdriver, with the fruity and herbal float of Galliano taking centre stage. It was created in the 1950s but its heyday was the golden age of disco in the 70s. It's ice cold and so breezily simple to put together – while it's perfect for a kitchen disco, try it as a pre-brunch sharpener. Galliano is pokey and a proper commitment to a great day of leisurely frolics ahead.

37.5ml (1¼oz) vodka

75ml (2½oz) freshly squeezed orange juice

Dash simple syrup (see page 11)

Dash orange bitters

15ml (½oz) Galliano

Ice: Cubed

Garnish: Orange slice

Equipment: Long bar spoon

Fill a glass with ice

Add all the ingredients except the Galliano

Stir gently to chill

Float the Galliano on top

Garnish with an orange slice

BALLET
RUSSE

Party drink! This hidden gem is a blackcurrant bonanza and a riot of refreshment. I once overheard a bartender in Copenhagen on a very late night exclaim: 'All purple drinks are the best drinks and that's a fact. Just ask people with purple faces – they know what they're doing.' It stuck with me: I can't decide if it's inspired or just ludicrous. Either way there's enough of a red-purple tint here to put the statement to the test. Maybe don't actually turn yourself purple, but your mood will certainly feel more colourful with a Ballet Russe in your hand.

60ml (2oz) vodka

22.5ml (¾oz) crème de cassis

30ml (1oz) freshly squeezed lime juice

7.5ml (¼oz) simple syrup (see page 11)

Ice: Cubed

Garnish: Lime wedge

Equipment: Cocktail shaker, strainer

Fill a shaker with ice

Add all the ingredients

Shake vigorously to chill

Strain into a chilled glass

Garnish with a lime wedge

SCREAMING ORGASM

It's always creamier and richer than you think. I'm tempted to leave it at that, because the facts speak for themselves here. This is filthy in the best possible way – full of indulgent pudding-like satisfaction with a generous dose of innuendo. And that's why I love it: it's got more kerbside appeal than a beachfront palace and the best time to sip it is pre-dinner. It slips down more easily than you might think and the creamy character sends the alcohol on a gentle upswing into your system, delivering a revved-up appetite within 30 minutes. A close second for me is sipping it tucked up on the sofa just for its sheer unwinding easiness. You may murmur the name, I just let the drink do the talking.

15ml (½oz) vodka

15ml (½oz) Baileys

15ml (½oz) Kahlua

15ml (½oz) amaretto

60ml (2oz) single (light) cream

Ice: Cubed

Garnish: Chocolate powder

Equipment: Cocktail shaker, strainer

Fill a shaker with ice

Add all the ingredients

Shake vigorously to chill

Strain into a glass filled with ice

Garnish with chocolate powder

The perfect embodiment of the 80s – a truly excessive cocktail from the era of excess.

Omit the vodka if you want a basic **Orgasm**.

PORNSTAR MARTINI

I have a number of bars on board cruise ships and the Pornstar Martini is without question the cocktail that is ordered the most. It's enjoyed a revival in recent years but as far as I'm concerned, this cocktail has never gone out of fashion, it will never go out of fashion. Although you may choose it for the name, it's the flavour that lures me – so scrumptious, unmissable and exotic. One of my favourite memories of ship-life drinks was a lost afternoon spent in my bar drifting off Spain's southern coast with the late comedian and national treasure Ronnie Corbett. Such a genial raconteur, and although this drink may not bring you his powers of storytelling, it's guaranteed to make you feel like you on your very best day – by which I mean, get making this drink for an instant taste of holiday.

45ml (1½oz) vanilla vodka

15ml (½oz) passion fuit liqueur

30ml (1oz) passion fruit purée

15ml (½oz) freshly squeezed lime juice

15ml (½oz) vanilla simple syrup (see page 11)

60ml (2oz) Champagne or sparkling wine

Ice: Cubed

Garnish: Passion fruit half

Equipment: Cocktail shaker, strainer

Fill a shaker with ice

Add all the ingredients except the sparkling wine

Shake vigorously to chill

Strain into a chilled glass

Garnish with half a passion fruit

Serve the Champagne or sparkling wine in a shot glass on the side

SEA
BREEZE

The Sea Breeze feels to me like it's healthy. I'm not going to say you should drink ten of them, but one never seems to do me any harm at home. The simplicity of building the drink is reflected in its easy, fruity charm. And you could totally pre-make the recipe in a jug for even simpler deployment. Sure, it invokes the beach feeling of kicking back in a lounger, and it owes some of its enduring success to clever marketing by Absolut Vodka and Ocean Spray. Fact is, it's super-straightforward to build in the glass and it tastes great. That's why it's an all-time classic.

45ml (1½oz) vodka

75ml (2½oz) cranberry juice

30ml (1oz) grapefruit juice

Ice: Cubed

Garnish: Lime wedge

Equipment: Long bar spoon

Fill a glass with ice

Add all the ingredients to the glass

Stir well to chill

Garnish with a lime wedge

Change the grapefruit juice to pineapple juice for a **Bay Breeze**.

For a **Madras** swap the grapefruit juice for orange juice (and add an orange slice to garnish).

SEX ON
THE BEACH

Fruit, exoticism, naughtiness – what's not to love? This is my version of the dangerously drinkable 1980s sweet cocktail. Sit back and think of 80s classics: big hair, bright colours, puffy dresses and a general air of bouffant. My hair at the time was emerging from its childhood pudding basin into long locks that I hoped had a surfy vibe, but in reality were more 'medieval page boy'. I made up for it in later years with a barnet that veered from buzzcut to Empire State height, all as varied as the iterations of this recipe, yet none quite so satisfying.

22.5ml (¾oz) vodka

22.5ml (¾oz) Midori

22.5ml (¾oz) Chambord

30ml (1oz) orange juice

30ml (1oz) cranberry juice

Ice: Cubed

Garnish: Orange-cherry sail

Equipment: Cocktail shaker, strainer

Fill a shaker with ice

Add all the ingredients

Shake vigorously to chill

Strain into a glass filled with ice

Garnish with an orange-cherry sail for a retro finish

There are lots of variations of Sex on the Beach – for example, you can also add 22.5ml (¾oz) peach schnapps instead of Midori.

FRENCH MARTINI

Some people say France is a hotbed of experimentation: I say in this case a little kinkiness leads to the straight and narrow. The Martini that isn't a Martini, this drink is worthy of the philosophical contemplations of Jean-Paul Sartre himself. Why do I love it? It's easy to make – and perhaps the simplest of all cocktails to customise. Try shifting the quantity of juice and dialling around the vodka and Chambord until you hit your sweet spot. This recipe is perfect for me, but you're the one making the drink: in the name of curiosity, experimentation is obligatory.

45ml (1½oz) vodka

15ml (½oz) Chambord

45ml (¾oz) pineapple juice

Ice: Cubed

Garnish: Pineapple wedge

Equipment: Cocktail shaker, strainer

Fill a shaker with ice

Add all the ingredients

Shake vigorously to chill

Strain into a chilled glass

Garnish with a pineapple wedge

Despite its name this isn't technically a Martini.

To make this a **Very French Martini** swap the vodka for Cognac.

Experiment with different flavour combinations by using vanilla or bison grass vodka.

SALTY DOG

Like all good salty dogs, this one has a twist in the tail. I love it with gin, but it's up to you whether to go with the classic vodka or not. This is a drink with proper sharp edges – think skiing on grapefruit wedges. Its massive citrus presence cuts through the moment and it's so simple to make. If you have the time and access to fruit, fresh pink grapefruit juice is sublime in season, but decent shop-bought stuff is perfectly fine the rest of the time. If you enjoy a Margarita, you'll love a Salty Dog.

45ml (1½oz) vodka

15ml (½oz) cherry liqueur

90ml (3oz) pink grapefruit juice

Ice: Cubed

Garnish: Salted rim

Equipment: Long bar spoon

Salt the rim of a glass

Fill with ice

Add all the ingredients

Stir gently to combine

Works equally well with gin.

Experiment by adding your favourite fruit bitters.

Omit the cherry liqueur and the salted rim to make a classic **Greyhound**.

SUNSTROKE

Much fruitier than you'd think and much less of a burn, this is ideal to cool off and kick back with when the mercury rises. I enjoyed a steady river of these on holiday in Skopelos one year as the kids leapt around and the days of gold poured from the sky. Sunstroke is one to master the proportions of, so that wherever you are in the world you can easily knock it up without blinking. The proportions in this recipe are as balanced as the hydrofoil that takes you from Skiathos to Skopelos, curling perfect blue ribbons of ocean as you head towards a gentle tan and one of these cool zingers. Drinking it with your shades on is mandatory – it definitely helps you to drift into the sunny vibes of this stunning cocktail. Suntan cream is optional.

37.5ml (1¼oz) vodka

22.5ml (¾oz) triple sec

45ml (¾oz) pink grapefruit juice

Ice: Cubed

Garnish: Orange twist

Equipment: Cocktail shaker, muddler and strainer

Fill a shaker with ice

Add all the ingredients

Shake vigorously to chill

Strain into a chilled glass

Garnish with an orange twist

A dash of grapefruit bitters can be added as an optional extra.

UNCLE VANYA

Aaaah, crème de mûre! The hidden blackberry elixir of rich, fruity sweetness. Another hidden gem for you: I'm a cousin of Hugo Weaving (Elrond in *Lord of the Rings*, Agent Smith in *The Matrix*) and much as I adore him in the movies – particularly *Priscilla, Queen of the Desert* – the production I most wanted to see him in was Chekhov's *Uncle Vanya*. I've always been fascinated by the vodka and emotion that flows in equal measure through the script, as it does through this recipe. The Sydney Theatre Company produced *Uncle Vanya* in 2010 with Hugo in the role of Astrov and Cate Blanchett as Elena and it was reprised in 2012 in New York, but due to work commitments I didn't make it to either run. A lasting regret – and no, the real reason I missed both runs is categorically not because I'd been drinking too many Uncle Vanyas! Aside from 'go and see your cousin in a play', the best advice I can give here is 'embrace the egg white'. You can always substitute it with aquafaba (the liquid from a tin of chickpeas), though I find the satin and silk foam of the egg white delivers the most gorgeous texture to this sweet, fruity cocktail.

37.5ml (1¼oz) vodka

22.5ml (¾oz) crème de mûre

22.5ml (¾oz) freshly squeezed lime juice

7.5ml (¼oz) simple syrup (see page 11)

½ an egg white (or 1 tbsp aquafaba)

Ice: Cubed

Garnish: Lime wedge

Equipment: Cocktail shaker, strainer

Fill a shaker with ice

Add all the ingredients

Shake vigorously to chill

Strain into a chilled glass

Garnish with a lime wedge

To make a **Katinka**, substitute the crème de mûre with apricot liqueur.

WOO WOO

Mix this in mere moments and feel the playful mood take hold. I'm a massive fan of *Friends* and whenever I order a Woo Woo I think of 'The One With Joey's Fridge'. Ross is controversially dating one of his students and planning a spring break trip, which causes Chandler to make a 'woo woo' sound whenever the idea is mentioned. This cocktail cannot fail to raise a grin and if you decided to make a large batch to top up glasses as you go, I'd encourage giggles, silliness and joyful laughter to accompany the occasion. A bit like your favourite episode of *Friends*.

30ml (1oz) vodka

30ml (1oz) peach schnapps

75ml (2½oz) cranberry juice

Ice: Cubed

Garnish: Lime wedge

Equipment: Bar spoon

Fill a glass with ice

Add all the ingredients

Stir to combine

Garnish with a lime wedge

SCREWDRIVER

Inexplicably underrated, the Screwdriver is an easy drink that has 24-hour appeal. Put simply, there is no wrong time or place for sipping a Screwdriver. Movie night? Sure. Party all day? You bet. Right now? Absolutely.

90ml (3oz) freshly squeezed orange juice

45ml (1½oz) vodka

2 dashes orange bitters

Ice: Cubed

Garnish: Orange slice

Fill a glass with ice

Add all the ingredients to the glass

Stir to combine (ideally with a bar spoon, but legend has it this was originally mixed with a screwdriver)

Garnish with an orange slice

This classic cocktail has to be made with freshly squeezed oranges. For a seasonal change use blood oranges instead of oranges.

Or try adding a dash of Aperol and a squeeze of lemon juice, and top with soda.

FRESH LEMONADE

How easy is Fresh Lemonade?! Serve this to anyone who pops round or to guests before a feast instead of a glass of fizz, and the effect is instantaneous. Here's where I hear the sacred voice of my dear friend and chef Gennaro Contaldo crooning in my ear, reminding me of the importance of choosing top-quality lemons, and while your average shop-bought will do fine here, if you really want that extra scented magic, seek out fruit from Italy's Amalfi Coast. They turn the freshness up to 11 – with a homemade cocktail this simple, it's well worth dialling up the deliciousness.

45ml (1½oz) vodka

22.5ml (¾oz) freshly squeezed lemon juice

15ml (½oz) simple syrup (see page 11)

Soda water, to top

Ice: Crushed

Garnish: Lemon wheel

Equipment: Long bar spoon

Fill a glass two-thirds with crushed ice

Add all the ingredients except the soda water

Churn gently to chill

Top with soda water and cap with crushed ice

Garnish with a wheel of lemon

Change citrus fruits for variations.

RASPBERRY WATKINS

'Raspberry Watkins' would be an excellent pen-name, to be signed with a flourish of a luxurious fountain pen. It's also the name of this drink, which stands for two of the greatest things in life:

1. Refreshment
2. All things pink

Lengthening the drink with soda brings refreshment to the frivolity of colour and fruit-fuelled dynamism of the grenadine-Chambord duet. You could deploy the Raspberry Watkins on romantic occasions, but every day should be a day when love is welcomed with open arms, so for me, this is the drink to pour at the merest hint of a sunbeam. If you're not wearing a coat, that instantly indicates that a Raspberry Watkins should be in your hand to bring some love to your heart.

37.5ml (1¼oz) vodka

22.5ml (¾oz) Chambord

15ml (½oz) freshly squeezed lime juice

7.5ml (¼oz) grenadine

Soda water, to top

Ice: Cubed

Garnish: Lime wedge

Equipment: Cocktail shaker, strainer

Fill a shaker with ice

Add all the ingredients except the soda water

Shake vigorously to chill

Strain into a glass filled with ice and top with soda water

Garnish with a lime wedge

GLACIER MINT

Mint is a flourishing upswing of scent and flavour that signifies summertime all year round. Green crème de menthe lurks around the fringes of acceptability with After Eight Mints and Wrigley's doublemint gum and I'm not sure why. If it's down to the lurid colour, then this cocktail is off the hook as I'm using white crème de menthe, which is great to have in your back pocket for things like quick mojitos too. And it tastes different from good old Fox's Glacier Mints; while those belong in the glovebox, this belongs in your facebox.

45ml (1½oz) vodka

15ml (½oz) white crème de cacao

15ml (½oz) white crème de menthe

Ice: Cubed

Garnish: Mint sprig

Equipment: Cocktail shaker, strainer

Fill a shaker with ice

Add all the ingredients

Shake vigorously to chill

Strain into a chilled glass

Garnish with a mint sprig

Essentially like drinking an After Eight.

Can also be built straight into a glass filled with ice for an on-the-rocks version.

GINGER SCRUFF

The hazelnut is my favourite nut of all time. I love the burnished colour of the shells, I can crack them without bursting a bicep and most of all I adore their creamy taste with characterful bite. Frangelico, a hazelnut liqueur, has stunning richness and is so extraordinarily mellow alongside the more vibrant lemon and ginger in this recipe – the interplay is phenomenal. Stick carefully to the proportions and this drink is a sweet ignition of powerful quenching. Countdown to make it in 3, 2, 1, NOW.

37.5ml (1¼oz) lemon vodka

22.5ml (¾oz) Frangelico

7.5ml (¼oz) freshly squeezed lemon juice

90ml (3oz) fiery ginger beer, to top

Ice: Crushed

Garnish: Lemon wedge

Equipment: Long bar spoon

Fill a glass two-thirds with crushed ice

Add all the ingredients except the ginger beer

Churn gently to chill

Top with ginger beer and cap with more crushed ice

CITRUS
CRUSH

Orange juice and orange vodka make me think of the scented blossom of southern Spain's orange trees – my favourite place to wander and waft in the splendour of it is Sanlúcar de Barrameda on the coast. This recipe is as close as you can get to that feeling of a small square at sunset with voices dispersing into bars and blossom on the breeze. And as ever, freshly squeezed juice is worth the elbow and effort – it delivers maximum zing and intense vibrancy.

45ml (1½oz) orange vodka

45ml (1½oz) cranberry juice

30ml (1oz) freshly squeezed orange juice

7.5ml (¼oz) freshly squeezed lime juice

7.5ml (¼oz) freshly squeezed lemon juice

Ice: Cubed and crushed

Garnish: Lime wedge

Equipment: Cocktail shaker, strainer

Fill a shaker with cubed ice

Add all the ingredients

Shake vigorously to chill

Strain into a glass filled with crushed ice

Garnish with a lime wedge

Lemon vodka works equally well.

PEACH CRUSH

Aah. The first time I made a Peach Crush I was in Pézenas in the south of France and my youngest daughter Lily spent a day walking around a market refusing to take off her swimming goggles so she'd be ready to dive in as soon as we got back to the pool. She also insisted we call her Brenda, but that's another story. We were winding our way through the peach stalls in the market and the scent has never left me from that day. So heady and delightful, a portal to a sweeter way of life. With a paper bag of them squished under my arm as we got home, I knocked up a Peach Crush and as Brenda toppled delightedly into the pool I fell in love with everything. Simple to make, divine to enjoy.

30ml (1oz) vodka

30ml (1oz) peach schnapps

60ml (2oz) cranberry juice

15ml (½oz) freshly squeezed lime juice

7.5ml (¼oz) simple syrup (see page 11)

Ice: Cubed and crushed

Garnish: Fresh peach slice

Equipment: Cocktail shaker, strainer

Fill a shaker with cubed ice

Add all the ingredients

Shake vigorously to chill

Strain into a glass filled with crushed ice

Garnish with a slice of peach

ROSE LEMONADE

Rose is the most underrated flavour in any drink. Its flavour is almost identical to its scent: sweet and heady enough to make you feel like it's springtime with every sip. Rather than a drink that's as sweet as honey, this drink has the lime to act as a vibrant scimitar, cutting through everything with a shard of citrus precision. And you'll notice I've gone for fresh lime juice here over lemon. Even though we're making Rose Lemonade, the exotic edge of lime works a charm with rose and has that little bit more zing to it to give the drink propulsion from the top of your tongue to the tips of your toes.

45ml (1½oz) vodka

22.5ml (¾oz) freshly squeezed lime juice

15ml (½oz) rose-flavoured simple syrup (see page 11)

Soda water, to top

Ice: Crushed

Garnish: Edible rose petal

Equipment: Long bar spoon

Fill a glass two-thirds with crushed ice

Add all the ingredients except the soda water

Top with soda water

Churn gently to chill and cap with crushed ice

Garnish with a rose petal

PEACHY KEEN

Golden and bubbly? This is like drinking the Oscars. The purity of vodka acts as a prism around the peach here, boosted by schnapps and enriched with purée. Peach schnapps is so handy to add fast flavour to cocktails and once you've found your favourite, you'll find the bottle doesn't hang around long. Just like this recipe, in fact! The Peachy Keen is the only drink you'll need to make you feel that life is riper than it strictly needs to be.

37.5ml (1¼oz) vodka

22.5ml (¾oz) peach schnapps

60ml (2oz) white peach purée

7.5ml (¼oz) freshly squeezed lime juice

Soda water, to top

6–8 mint leaves

Ice: Cubed

Garnish: Mint sprig

Equipment: Muddler, cocktail shaker, strainer

Muddle mint in a shaker then fill with ice

Add all the ingredients except the soda water

Shake vigorously to chill

Strain into a glass filled with ice

Top with soda water

Add a sprig of mint to garnish

LONG ISLAND ICED TEA

So many ingredients and yet so singularly refreshing. An outrage of a drink that belongs in the lexicon of every guide to the good life. While vodka doesn't dominate here, it certainly underpins the tapestry of balance with seamless class. Cool vodka always makes me think of mountains and brooks – its pristine clarity lets all radiant colours shine through. In this case the cocktail's tea-like tone sometimes leads people to suggest that it was a Prohibition drink designed to disguise the liquor. I prefer to think of it as an 80s classic along with big hair, ghetto blasters and neon socks. I'm still just as partial today to a neon sock as I am to a Long Island Iced Tea. Both jump with intensity and the booze is spectacularly poised to bring the perfectly calculated level of carefree class. One sip and your moment, like the cocktail, becomes iconic.

15ml (½oz) vodka

15ml (½oz) light rum

15ml (½oz) gin

15ml (½oz) silver tequila

15ml (½oz) triple sec

30ml (1oz) freshly squeezed lemon juice

15ml (½oz) simple syrup (see page 11)

30ml (1oz) cola, to top

Ice: Cubed

Garnish: Lemon wedge

Equipment: Cocktail shaker, strainer

Fill a shaker with ice

Add all the ingredients except the cola

Shake vigorously to chill

Strain into a glass filled with ice and top with the cola

Garnish with a lemon wedge

Replace the cola with cranberry juice to make a **Long Beach Iced Tea**.

Replace the cola with pineapple juice to make an **Hawaiian Iced Tea**.

For a **Tokyo Tea** replace the cola with lemon-lime soda and the triple sec with **Midori**.

PINEAPPLE SNAPPER

Pineapples are inherently fun. Their shape, vibrant fruity colour and sharp sweetness catapult them to the top of the list of fruit most likely to throw some secret shapes when nobody's looking. Great as a garnish, even better in a drink, it pairs brilliantly with lemon vodka, ginger and even orgeat (you say it 'or-zhat'), which is a heady combo of almond and orange flower water and sends you thirst class to the shores of Exotica Shoals, the imaginary place where I like to dream of endless Pineapple Snapper sunsets. Shake and strain this beauty and slip away to your very own slice of paradise.

37.5ml (1¼oz) lemon vodka

15ml (½oz) Stone's Ginger Wine

30ml (1oz) pineapple Juice

15ml (½oz) freshly squeezed lime juice

7.5ml (¼oz) honey simple syrup (see page 11)

Dash orgeat

Soda water, to top

Ice: Crushed

Garnish: Pineapple wedge

Equipment: Cocktail shaker, strainer

Fill a shaker with ice

Add all the ingredients except the soda water

Shake vigorously to chill

Strain into a glass filled with ice

Top with soda water and garnish with a pineapple wedge

GIN

The gin balloon keeps rising to the sky. It flows in clear rivers from distilleries the world over; the nuances, subtleties and variation of gin are as eclectic as the make-up, moods and music of the great David Bowie himself. Gin's roots are entangled with juniper's medieval fame for medicinal magic as much as the notorious craze for it in the 1700s that earned it the nickname Mother's Ruin. Happily, today gin's story is far jollier – and some key concepts will ensure your cocktails are as tantalising as they are consistent.

Gin begins with a neutral, clear base spirit commonly made of wheat or barley which is redistilled with natural ingredients such as seeds, fruits and herbs known as 'botanicals'. The most important of these is juniper, which always gives the classic headline flavour of aromatic freshness that gin is prized for. Water is added to dilute ready for final bottling. The skill of blenders and brands is in maintaining consistency month to month and year to year over the whole process. Considering all the possible ingredients in gin, from roots to berries, peel to bark, all naturally grown, some foraged from the wild and inevitably subject to the conditions of each season, the whole process can be a bit of a Hogwarts staircase, with every step towards consistency continuously shifting.

Some distillers submerge and steep their botanicals in the process, others prefer to leave the flavour infusion to vapours, hanging the botanicals in baskets – and sometimes distillers combine the two methods. With all the complexities of creating gin, all you really need to worry about is the style that best suits your taste. For most of these cocktail recipes, a classic London dry gin will work best; however, there are certain instances where

Old Tom is worth considering if you fancy deepening your journey.

London dry gin As an all-rounder to catch decent-quality aromatics delivering flavour during distillation, this is your must-have bottle. With juniper leading the classic phalanx of flavours, London gin only uses natural ingredients with nothing permitted to be added after distillation and no sweeteners, which ensures its bright, zesty, 'dry' style. It can be made globally as it's a style rather than a geographical definition; alongside juniper, classic botanicals include coriander seeds, citrus peel of some form and angelica root.

Old Tom gin is generally a little sweeter than London dry, and works a charm in drinks such as the Tom Collins to round out the tingling, sour edges.

While there are plenty of variations and, of course, flavoured gins, I'd keep your choice as simple as possible and focus on finding the bottle of London dry that thrills you most. Stick to using that one in all these cocktails. I will, however, give a fond mention to **gin de Mahón**, which is made in Menorca and offers something a little unique and historic. One such product, Xoriguer (pronounced 'shore-ee-gayr'), is an aromatic powerhouse, and always reels me into a reverie of peppery, minty, herbaceous delight. It's unique, and for a characterful gin and tonic it delivers a walloping hoof of fine flavour. It includes a base spirit of wine alcohol in wood-fired copper stills, but the recipe is a closely guarded secret even to this day. All I can reveal for certain is that in my opinion it does joyful justice to juniper.

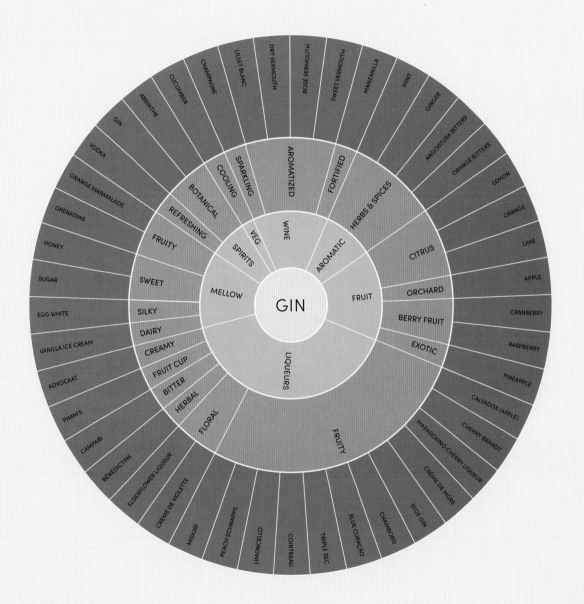

GIBSON/ CLASSIC GIN MARTINI

A Gibson is only a Gibson if it contains onions. And I am a fiend for a pickled onion. I peel my own, add various spices and leave them for weeks or months to develop a spiky punch. The trouble with my onions is they are simply too big to float in a Gibson. A little cocktail onion with silver skin is called for. Looks great and is milder than my pickled spice grenades.

The proportions of gin to dry vermouth are always hotly debated in a Martini, as is the type of dry vermouth and of course the type of gin. However, my foolproof rule of thumb – 75ml of gin to 15ml of dry vermouth – is failsafe and delivers all the flavour of gin enhanced by dry vermouth without any overlapping or jostling for centre stage. Seamless refreshment abounds in a cocktail orbiting two very small orbs.

75ml (2½oz) gin

15ml (½oz) dry vermouth

Ice: Cubed

Garnish: Cocktail onions

Equipment: Cocktail shaker, strainer, long bar spoon

Fill a shaker with ice

Add all the ingredients

Stir gently to combine

Strain into a chilled glass

Garnish with 2 speared cocktail onions

For a **Classic Gin Martini** swap the cocktail onion for an olive or lemon twist garnish.

ANGELS IN
THE COCKPIT

I invented this cocktail in the name of ease. I love the idea that angels could take a breather from flying with their wings by popping into a jet plane and taking the helm for a while or just kicking back and raiding the duty free. I imagine this drink would be in their hands as they did.

Calvados, peach schnapps and gin are not necessarily the first drinks you might send towards the same destination, yet they seamlessly unite so impressively that you barely notice you've taken off. You certainly won't know you've landed – and it turns out baggage reclaim is filled with bags of fun.

30ml (1oz) gin

30ml (1oz) Calvados

30ml (1oz) peach schnapps

Ice: Cubed

Garnish: Peach wedge

Equipment: Long bar spoon

Fill a glass with ice

Add all the ingredients

Stir gently to combine

Garnish with a peach wedge

NEGRONI

The Negroni is one of my all-time favourite cocktails and a bottle of Campari is never further than arm's reach in my life. I even considered naming my dog Campari until I realised Busby suited him much better. In my view the Negroni is too often thought of as an after-dinner drink. True, its flavours are powerful with the sweet vermouth, bitter Campari and vibrant gin delivering a trilogy of intense, harmonious power. However, I always say 'never not Negroni' – the point being, cold Negronis are for all hours of the day and night. They are great revivers for a flagging mood, they are a great opening pitch for a top time, and they're surprisingly delicious with intense, spicy nibbles such as olives laced with lemon, chilli and garlic. The only thing that could possibly improve this recipe is making it while wearing a T-shirt that says 'never not Negroni'.

22.5ml (¾oz) gin

22.5ml (¾oz) Campari

22.5ml (¾oz) sweet vermouth

Ice: Cubed

Garnish: Orange twist

Equipment: Long bar spoon

Fill a glass with ice

Pour all the ingredients into the glass

Stir gently to combine

Garnish with an orange twist

Replace the Campari with Jägermeister for an unusual if outrageous alternative.

For an orange kick replace the Campari with Aperol and substitute the sweet vermouth for dry.

Replace the gin with prosecco to make a **Sbagliato** – a lengthened version of the Negroni, and a cocktail I once particularly enjoyed on a memorably warm day in April with my friend Matt on the rooftop of the Dorchester hotel.

SLOEGRONI

This cocktail is a very simple way of switching a couple of ingredients in a Negroni for sloe gin – and it's well worth using the rosé vermouth to allow the sloes to shine more brightly. The Sloegroni has a fruity depth and is a little less bitter than a Negroni. I love it for its sumptuous resonance, like a purple sunset gently gargling with goodwill.

22.5ml (¾oz) gin

22.5ml (¾oz) sloe gin

22.5ml (¾oz) Campari

22.5ml (¾oz) rosé vermouth

Ice: Cubed

Garnish: Orange slice

Equipment: Long bar spoon

Fill a glass with ice

Add all the ingredients

Stir gently to combine

Garnish with an orange slice

If you don't have rosé vermouth, just use sweet vermouth as you would in a Negroni.

GIMLET

An absolute classic and very easy to make. If I was a stout warrior in a fighting-fantasy movie I would call myself Gimlet. My axe would be as mighty as my carpet of a blonde beard, which I would tie around my waist like an apron whenever I make this cocktail.

The Gimlet involves possibly the simplest but most enduringly vibrant addition to gin. That's why I love truly great cocktails – they don't need to be complicated to be world class. I reckon lime juice is essential to get a full jolt out of the gin and into your life. While its dose of Dutch courage may not take you to battle, it'll certainly be as sweet as a peacetime banquet. And it's so easy to create and share.

75ml (2½oz) gin

15ml (½oz) freshly squeezed lime juice

15ml (½oz) simple syrup (see page 11)

Ice: Cubed

Garnish: Lime twist

Equipment: Cocktail shaker, strainer

Fill a shaker with ice

Add all the ingredients

Shake vigorously to chill

Strain into a chilled glass

Garnish with a lime twist

You can swap the gin for vodka.

VESPER

The general rule of thumb is to stir and not shake spirit-only drinks. However, the Vesper is a notable exception. Just make sure you fine-strain when serving to remove any ice shards.

This drink was famously invented by author Ian Fleming and was James Bond's choice of drink in the novel *Casino Royale*. The original recipe called for the use of Kina Lillet but as that's no longer available most recipes use Lillet Blanc.

The Vesper made a memorable appearance in the movie version of *Casino Royale* when Daniel Craig's 007 simultaneously creates and orders the cocktail and his fellow gamblers follow suit, much to the annoyance of the villain, Le Chiffre.

It's true there's an allure to it, and there is a risk that once you make a Vesper everybody within sipping distance will be wanting one. No bad thing if you're in the mood for company, otherwise keep your cards close to your chest and sip with discretion.

60ml (2oz) gin

22.5ml (¾oz) vodka

15ml (½oz) Lillet Blanc

Ice: Cubed

Garnish: Lemon twist

Equipment: Cocktail shaker, strainer

Fill a shaker with ice

Add all the ingredients

Shake vigorously to chill

Strain into a chilled glass

Garnish with a lemon twist

FRENCH 75

This cocktail is named after the 75mm field gun used by the French and known for its power and kick in World War I. It's often thought of as a detonation of a drink, but to my mind the French 75 is a cocktail of elegance and sophistication. Champagne always elevates a simple cocktail into a classic and with a French 75 in your hand, sipping at home feels more like swooshing around a ballroom than battling with artillery. Either way, I suppose you could say the perfection of a dance, a duel or a drink is all in the precision.

30ml (1oz) gin

15ml (½oz) freshly squeezed lemon juice

15ml (½oz) simple syrup (see page 11)

90ml (3oz) Champagne, to top

Ice: Cubed

Garnish: Lemon twist

Equipment: Cocktail shaker, strainer

Fill a shaker with ice

Add all the ingredients except the Champagne

Shake vigorously to chill

Strain into a glass filled with ice and top with the Champagne

Garnish with a lemon twist

You can use your favourite sparkling wine. It doesn't have to be Champagne – you can even use sparkling cider to make a **French Harvest**.

TOM COLLINS

'Tom Collins' would be my code name if ever I was a superspy. 'It's so overt it's covert,' as Sherlock Holmes once said. Traditionally made with Old Tom gin (slightly less dry than London gin), it's a refreshing glass of genius. In essence a Tom Collins is a gin sour that's stretched out with soda, and it's so popular it's even got a glass named after it. It's a simple classic to master and one that you can customise at will – the Collins family of drinks is seemingly a never-ending combination of spirit with sour, sweet and soda. For some reason I always associate a Tom Collins with sipping it in the sun after a leisurely game of tennis but, in truth, great moments to enjoy a Tom Collins include brunch, late afternoon or whenever you are on a quest for a quenching. Tennis racket is optional.

60ml (2oz) gin

22.5ml (¾oz) freshly squeezed lemon juice

15ml (½oz) simple syrup (see page 11)

60ml (2oz) soda water, to top

Ice: Cubed

Garnish: Lemon wheel

Equipment: Cocktail shaker, strainer

Fill a shaker with ice

Add all the ingredients except the soda water

Shake vigorously to chill

Strain into a glass filled with ice and top with soda water

Garnish with a lemon wheel

To make a **Raspberry Collins** simply muddle a small handful of raspberries at the bottom of a shaker before adding the ice.

This drink also works well if you swap the gin for brandy.

QUEEN BEE

As a former beekeeper, I have great affection for those industrious little pollinators, and honey is a tremendous ingredient in cocktails. It's important, I think, to use it sparingly as it's a surprisingly powerful flavour that can dominate more delicate ones, and that's why the proportions are so key in this buzzing beauty of a drink. Citrus and honey are a classic combination; lemon and orange here both give support to gin's naturally upbeat botanicals.

This is a cocktail that transports you from your living room to the very living soul of a country garden in full bloom. And since I always used to name my queen bees after wonderful women in my life, this cocktail is nicknamed the Dinkel Drink, after my wife's marvellous family name: Dinkel.

60ml (2oz) gin

22.5ml (¾oz) freshly squeezed lemon juice

15ml (½oz) honey simple syrup (see page 11)

7.5ml (¼oz) orange juice (optional)

Ice: Cubed

Garnish: Lemon twist

Equipment: Cocktail shaker, strainer

Fill a shaker with ice

Add all the ingredients

Shake vigorously to chill

Strain into a chilled glass

Garnish with an orange twist

Use a honey simple syrup for this recipe as it's hard to get honey to mix well in cold drinks.

BRONX

The story behind this cocktail claims it was dreamed up around the time of the opening of the Bronx Zoological Park in 1899. What I know for certain is that vermouth and gin are magnificently like-minded, with herbs, spices and botanicals amplifying and orchestrating their taste and complexity. Freshly squeezed orange juice frames their nuances with an immediate fanfare of vibrancy and vigour. I always think of this cocktail as a Martini maxed out with orange juice. And that's why the Bronx is a drink I always love to pour at brunch – after you've had a few, try saying 'brunch' and you might find it sounds a little more like 'Bronx'.

45ml (1½oz) gin

15ml (½oz) dry vermouth

15ml (½oz) sweet vermouth

30ml (1oz) freshly squeezed orange juice

Dash orange bitters

Ice: Cubed

Garnish: Orange twist

Equipment: Cocktail shaker, strainer

Fill a shaker with ice

Add all the ingredients

Shake vigorously to chill

Strain into a chilled glass

Garnish with an orange twist

Use blood orange to make a **Bloody Bronx**.

MARTINEZ

The Martinez is a precursor to the Martini, created in the late 1800s and a must-taste for any Martini fan. And, for that matter, fans of the Manhattan. It is also a drink that always makes me think of my granny.

My grandmother was a vicar known as Granny Pip (her dog was called Pip). One of her favourite drinks was sweet vermouth on ice. I vividly recall watching the hypnotic, orangey trails of colour lacing around the melting ice on a sunny day. It's an amazing drink straight-up, especially for red wine fans. I raise my Martinez to her love of such rich, punchy flavours, and this is my nod to her stamina and love of sweet vermouth.

60ml (2oz) gin

22.5ml (¾oz) sweet vermouth

7.5ml (¼oz) maraschino cherry liqueur

2 dashes Angostura Bitters

Ice: Cubed

Garnish: Orange twist

Equipment: Cocktail shaker, strainer

Fill a shaker with ice

Add all the ingredients

Stir gently to combine

Strain into a chilled glass

Garnish with an orange twist

AVIATION

Crème de violette is a rare ingredient yet one that belongs at the very heart of this cracking cocktail, a riff on the Gin Sour. The scent of violets that appears in the countryside around spring is as distinctive and resonant as Dolly Parton's voice and one of the great treasures of the natural world. The splendour of violets rises all the way through this cocktail up to the sky as the Aviation lifts you and your guests into the heavens. And that delicate colour is an echo of clear skies on the brightest day.

Aromatic, easy and very impressive to serve as a surprising treat, this classic cocktail dating back to the early 1900s still wows with minimum of fuss. In the first few years of its existence, aviation was only available for the super-rich. My version of this cocktail is designed to send everybody soaring.

60ml (2oz) gin

15ml (½oz) maraschino cherry liqueur

15ml (½oz) crème de violette

15ml (½oz) freshly squeezed lemon juice

Ice: Cubed

Garnish: Lemon twist

Equipment: Cocktail shaker, strainer

Fill a shaker with ice

Add all the ingredients

Shake vigorously to chill

Strain into a chilled glass

Garnish with a lemon twist

GIN
RICKEY

This is quite a dry, tart drink but despite the lack of sugar it has the balance of duelling fencers on a highwire of lime peel.

If you're a fan of sharp citrus flavours, this is the drink for you. I would almost describe its flavour as similar to the piercing, bright sound of an unexpected triangle dinging – there's a tension to its zing and it's one to wake up to with a sense of wonder.

Gin's clarity is reflected in its vibrancy, which here is propelled into high gear by the lime juice. It was named in a Washington, DC, bar after a Colonel Rickey who moved in political circles at the time (1880s). Apparently he always insisted on lime as his citrus of choice; it's worth comparing it to the Collins family of drinks, which are traditionally made with lemon. Feel free to add more simple syrup to round out the lime, but personally I like my Rickeys to taste a little more risky.

45ml (1½oz) gin

15ml (½oz) freshly squeezed lime juice

7.5ml (¼oz) simple syrup (see page 11)

60ml (2oz) soda water, to top

Ice: Cubed

Garnish: Lime twist

Equipment: Long bar spoon

Fill a glass with ice

Add all the ingredients except the soda water

Stir gently to combine

Top with the soda water

Garnish with a lime twist

DIAMOND GIN FIZZ

Fizz always feels like fun, and the lengthening of gin with Champagne and syrup in this cocktail is designed to take you to the brighter side of being.

The Diamond Gin Fizz has the unique appeal of being as classy as it is informal, and it looks as impressive as it tastes. With the purity, clarity and sparkle of a diamond, it's as gratifying as drinking liquid treasure. Unleash your inner sparkle!

60ml (2oz) gin

30ml (1oz) freshly squeezed lemon juice

15ml (½oz) simple syrup (see page 11)

Dash orange bitters

Champagne, to top

Ice: Cubed

Garnish: Lemon wheel

Equipment: Cocktail shaker, strainer

Fill a shaker with ice

Add all the ingredients except the Champagne

Shake vigorously to chill

Strain into a glass filled with ice and top with Champagne

Garnish with a lemon wheel

As with any recipes using Champagne, you can swap it out for your favourite sparkling wine.

ENGLISH
GARDEN

This works well with a lighter, more floral gin rather than a classic, juniper-driven dry one. Mighty juniper shares the stage here with scented botanicals, which combine to emphasise the fragrant elderflower liqueur. Elderflower grows wild around my house like bridal bouquets for the birds; as apples on the trees start to swell this is the perfect cocktail to sip al fresco and admire it all. There's something splendid about the way that ingredients for gin grow all around the world – it's a spirit that could almost be described as a liquid garden. All that love from the landscape laced into one bottle: something to reflect on as you prepare your English Garden, which, by the way, is also stunning as a treat to get your appetite going for cakes and afternoon tea.

60ml (2oz) gin

22.5ml (¾oz) St-Germain elderflower liqueur

15ml (½oz) freshly squeezed lime juice

75ml (2½oz) cloudy apple juice

Ice: Cubed

Garnish: Cucumber slice and lime wedge

Equipment: Cocktail shaker, strainer

Fill a shaker with ice

Add all the ingredients

Shake vigorously to chill

Strain into a glass filled with ice

Garnish with a slice of cucumber and a lime wedge

GIN
GENIE

There are many cocktails out there with this name, all very different.

No need to rub your lamp for it though, the genie is already out of the bottle. Marvellous Midori blends with spicy ginger beer to transport your taste buds on a magic carpet ride across the horizons of expectation. A Gin Genie is super-easy to prepare: stirring gently to avoid too much dilution is the key to concocting this wish fulfiller.

The inspiration for my Gin Genie came in a Florida bar while I was filming a series about craft beer. When I tasted it, I instantly wanted to murmur, 'You ain't never had a friend like me...' With my version of this tasty tantaliser, you'll be best friends forever.

45ml (1½oz) gin

22.5ml (¾oz) Midori

15ml (½oz) freshly squeezed lime juice

75ml (2½oz) fiery ginger beer, to top

Ice: Cubed

Garnish: Lime wedge

Equipment: Long bar spoon

Fill a glass with ice

Add all the ingredients except the ginger beer

Stir gently to combine

Top with the ginger beer and stir once more to mix

Garnish with a lime wedge

PIMM'S
ROYALE

Ah, Pimm's! When will they hire me to dress in a silly costume at the head of a marching band like a majorette infused with human sunbeams and hose the world in the magic of Pimm's? I have marched to the beautiful beat of Pimm's all my life and remain a regular fan of its reliably stylish yet gently eccentric spicy blend. You can mix it with lemonade and chop some fruit into it or boost the bubbles with Champagne and crank up the gin for a royal treat. The proportions in my Royale recipe romp to the coronation of limitless luxury – and this is a party to which you are personally invited. I shall be coming dressed as a majorette, but your dress code is entirely up to you. I may even toss my baton.

45ml (1½oz) Pimm's No 1

15ml (½oz) gin

7.5ml (¼oz) simple syrup (see page 11)

7.5ml (¼oz) freshly squeezed lemon juice

Champagne, to top

Ice: Cubed

Garnish: Mint sprig, cucumber slices and quartered strawberry

Equipment: Long bar spoon

Add all the garnishes and ingredients except the Champagne to a glass

Stir gently to combine

Add ice

Top with Champagne and stir gently again

CLOVER CLUB

A classic whose roots are lost in the mists of time. Fluffed out with the egg white, this is a silken, rampant salute to the joy of raspberry, with soaring lemon juice and gin's pitch-perfect vibrancy. If you're a fan of the Pisco Sour, this outrageously easy-drinking cocktail is the one for you. It's an ingenious concoction, and if you wish you can replace the egg white with a similar quantity (around 1 tbsp) of aquafaba – the liquid from a tin of chickpeas. In this case though, I'd urge you embrace the egg white for its silky, glossy gorgeousness.

45ml (1½oz) gin

15ml (½oz) freshly squeezed lemon juice

15ml (½oz) raspberry syrup

½ an egg white

Ice: Cubed

Garnish: Orange twist

Equipment: Cocktail shaker, strainer

Dry shake (see page 211) all the ingredients in a cocktail shaker to emulsify the egg white

Fill the shaker with ice

Shake vigorously to chill

Strain into a chilled glass

Garnish with an orange twist

GIN & JUICE

This is a gorgeous gift of a drink to pre-make for parties – it's a shortcut to celebration. While I do encourage experimenting with your own juices, I am always lured to bright zestiness rather than anything too rich – it complements gin's zing. For balancing flavour and colour, cranberry, orange and pineapple offer as much unity and iconic appeal as the Three Musketeers.

60ml (2oz) gin

30ml (1oz) pineapple juice

30ml (1oz) orange juice

30ml (1oz) cranberry juice

Ice: Cubed

Garnish: Pineapple wedge

Equipment: Cocktail shaker, strainer

Fill a shaker with ice

Add all the ingredients

Shake vigorously to chill

Strain into a glass filled with ice

Garnish with a pineapple wedge

You can pick any combination of juices you like!

LEAPFROG

This is a brilliant drink that works with most styles of gin. It's perhaps more natural to think of pairing rum and ginger, with their sweet, spicy affinity. However, gin and ginger ale sharpened by lemon juice are just epic in their scope of riotous refreshment. This Leapfrog recipe epitomises fabulous flavour with minimum fuss. Sipping it makes me feel like I'm a buccaneer embarking on an adventure to the Islands of Amazement – there's always an extra spring in my stride with Leapfrog on the horizon.

60ml (2oz) gin

15ml (½oz) freshly squeezed lemon juice

90ml (3oz) ginger ale, to top

Ice: Cubed

Garnish: Lemon wedge

Equipment: Long bar spoon

Fill a glass with ice

Add all the ingredients except the ginger ale

Stir gently to combine

Top with the ginger ale

Garnish with a lemon wedge

Omit the lemon juice to make a **Gin Buck**.

Swap lemon juice for lime juice to make a **Dragonfly**.

Swap the gin for Irish whiskey to make an **Irish Buck**.

ORANGE BLOSSOM

Orange has always been my favourite colour. A sunset, the peel of the fruit, a shadow cast through a jar of marmalade: I adore it in all its guises. I also adore the scent of orange blossom, a treat I fleetingly enjoyed on occasional visits to southern Spain in the springtime. Orange blossom in the air offers a dreamy, sweetening distance between time and intent. It makes me dawdle. There's always an excuse to slow down and dwell more deeply when orange blossom hangs in the air – and this drink does the same. It is an invocation to time off and well worth creating. Rather than say it's a favourite, I shall merely say that this cocktail is even more scrumptious than you imagine it might be.

45ml (1½oz) gin

15ml (½oz) triple sec

45ml (1½oz) orange juice

15ml (½oz) freshly squeezed lime juice

7.5ml (¼oz) grenadine

Ice: Cubed

Garnish: Orange twist

Equipment: Cocktail shaker, strainer

Fill a shaker with ice

Add all the ingredients

Shake vigorously to chill

Strain into a glass filled with ice

Garnish with an orange twist

Pour the mix into a Champagne flute and top with sparkling wine to make a **Blossom Royale**.

FOGHORN

Like any good foghorn this cuts through the mizzle and comes straight to the point. It guides you away from danger and into a harbour of refreshment. Even as you rest at anchor, one Foghorn is never enough. In fact, if all the foghorns in the world were sounding at the same time in salute to you, that would pretty much have the same memorable impact as this drink does. Set your course for the sound of safety and this cocktail of calm and calibre.

60ml (2oz) gin

15ml (½oz) freshly squeezed lime juice

120ml (4oz) fiery ginger beer, to top

Ice: Cubed

Garnish: Lime wedge

Equipment: Cocktail shaker, strainer

Fill a shaker with ice

Add all the ingredients except the ginger beer

Stir gently to combine

Strain into a glass filled with ice

Top with the ginger beer

Garnish with a lime wedge

Old Tom gin is the best to use in this cocktail for its generous, round flavour – London Dry is more shrill, but totally fine to use if Old Tom is elusive.

PINK GIN

Pink gin is so popular and people spend a fortune on bottles with various additions of fruit-fuelled colour. However, the simplest method of all is to find the gin of your dreams and add three or four dashes of Angostura Bitters. I always love to balance that kick with a dash of simple syrup to smooth the assembly into seamless splendour. My uncle Tom always enjoyed a version of this Pink Gin back in the 1980s in his Northumberland home and he would often throw a few dried juniper berries into his ice-packed cut-crystal glass. I always thought he was a rather classy gent, and even though I'm using a lemon twist in my version, let's raise our glasses to the uniqueness of all those we admire – in my case, Uncle Tom.

60ml (2oz) gin

3–4 dashes Angostura Bitters

Dash simple syrup (see page 11)

Ice: Cubed

Garnish: Lemon twist

Equipment: Cocktail shaker, strainer

Fill a shaker with ice

Add all the ingredients

Stir gently to combine

Strain into a chilled glass

Garnish with a lemon twist

For a longer drink, pour into a tall glass filled with ice and top with tonic or pink lemonade.

IONA MARBLE

I love this cocktail, which I created for the launch of P&O Cruises' ship Iona. I tried to give a nod to the green marble that's found on the Scottish island of Iona, as well as reflect the pristine character that stone offers – the clean finish also reminds me of being at sea. The saline touch of dry sherry plus wine seemed a great choice to bind with the sweet zing of triple sec and lemon juice, all rounded off with simple syrup and glorified with gin. Here's to sailing on the high seas of great taste.

45ml (1½oz) gin

15ml (½oz) fino or manzanilla (dry) sherry

15ml (½oz) triple sec

30ml (1oz) freshly squeezed lemon juice

7.5ml (¼oz) simple syrup (see page 11)

Ice: Cubed

Garnish: Lemon twist

Equipment: Cocktail shaker, strainer

Fill a shaker with ice

Add all the ingredients

Shake vigorously to chill

Strain into a chilled glass

Garnish with a lemon twist

BRAMBLE

It may feel counterintuitive to pair the bounty of the hedgerow – the blackberry (with its luxuriant, sweet fragrance and deep colour) – with the clarity and brightness of gin. However, in this cocktail, it's what goes in the middle that counts, and the simple syrup and lemon juice act as a golden chain linking paradise with heaven on earth. A divine drink elevating the blackberry to its brambly zenith.

45ml (1½oz) gin

30ml (1oz) freshly squeezed lemon juice

15ml (½oz) simple syrup (see page 11)

15ml (½oz) crème de mûre

Ice: Crushed

Garnish: Blackberries and lemon slice

Equipment: Long bar spoon

Fill a glass two-thirds with crushed ice

Add all the ingredients except the crème de mûre

Stir gently to combine

Cap with more crushed ice and gently drizzle over the crème de mûre so it seeps down through the ice

Garnish with a blackberry or two and a slice of lemon

SHIMMYING TO NANTUCKET

For this recipe, I was originally trying to come up with a seaside cocktail for gin, and all I could think about was eating ice cream. My favourite thing at the seaside is raspberry ripple ice cream. Once I started thinking about raspberry syrup and a scoop of vanilla ice cream, it seemed inevitable that lemon juice, limoncello and gin would brighten up this cocktail like a rising sun glittering over the ocean in a cascade of diamonds. Sip this and life really is a beach.

45ml (1½oz) gin

15ml (½oz) limoncello

15ml (½oz) raspberry syrup

15ml (½oz) freshly squeezed lemon juice

Soda water, to top

1 scoop vanilla ice cream, to float

Ice: Cubed

Equipment: Cocktail shaker, strainer

Fill a shaker with ice

Add all the ingredients except the soda water and ice cream

Shake vigorously to chill

Strain into a chilled glass and top with soda water.

Float the ice cream on top of the cocktail

THE
FEATHER STEP

Light on its feet. Uplifting in flavour. As scented as skydiving into a giant bridal bouquet and just as joyful. The Feather Step is your fast-track pass to merriment. I love making them to celebrate romance, but don't just save them for Valentine's Day: make every day a day you love.

30ml (1oz) gin

15ml (½oz) St-Germain elderflower liqueur

15ml (½oz) freshly squeezed lemon juice

7.5ml (¼oz) elderflower syrup

Champagne, to top

Ice: Cubed

Garnish: Lemon twist

Equipment: Cocktail shaker, strainer

Fill a shaker with ice

Add all the ingredients except the Champagne

Shake vigorously to chill

Strain into a chilled flute and top with Champagne

Garnish with a lemon twist

MONKEY GLAND

A classic cocktail from the 1920s, named after some dodgy scientific experiments which we'll gloss over here. If you're curious, look up Serge Voronoff – but I'd advise focusing solely on the drink instead, which is far more palatable.

Absinthe is always to be used sparingly to avoid any monkey business – it has the ability to overpower the constellation of bright gin, zippy orange juice and sweet grenadine. I've been a little more generous in my measures of the fruity flavours in my Monkey Gland than some more classic iterations, preferring a more lavish dose of invigoration with a fuller flavour. I find this drink burns more brightly in the memory when it's savoured with steady sips.

60ml (2oz) gin

30ml (1oz) freshly squeezed orange juice

7.5ml (¼oz) grenadine

2 dashes absinthe

Ice: Cubed

Garnish: Orange twist

Equipment: Cocktail shaker, strainer

Fill a shaker with ice

Add all the ingredients except the absinthe

Shake vigorously to chill

Rinse the inside of a chilled glass with absinthe then discard the excess

Strain the contents of the shaker into the absinthe-rinsed glass

Garnish with an orange twist

FLUFFY DUCK

In this drink, gin takes equal billing headlining opposite advocaat, which I reckon is among the most underrated ingredients in cocktail history. Perhaps it's the colour, thickness or sweetness; the key, though, is to know how to use it, in what quantity, and when. I owe my fondness for advocaat to my friend Anatol who, in my eighteenth year, introduced me to its powers on a trip to Cambridge when he judiciously blended it into a range of spectacular cocktails. I've come to realise since then that advocaat is rather like the music of Pat Metheny – underappreciated and altogether magical. Just check out 'Sunlight' on his album *Secret Story* for an eternally charming toe-tapper. Just like the egg-based Dutch beverage, it's a little treat for every now and again. In this playful cocktail, the colour and fluffiness is thanks to advocaat; the triple sec and orange juice take care of the chorus of sweet citrus, while gin mingles like a bright superstar tumbling into an equanimous, soulful assembly. Just like Pat Metheny at the forefront of his jazzy band.

45ml (1½oz) gin

45ml (1½oz) advocaat

30ml (1oz) triple sec

30ml (1oz) orange juice

Soda water, to top

Ice: Cubed

Garnish: Orange-cherry sail (or a small rubber duck if you have one)

Equipment: Cocktail shaker, strainer

Fill a shaker with ice

Add all the ingredients except the soda water

Shake vigorously to chill

Strain into a glass filled with ice and top with soda water

Garnish with an orange-cherry sail

PINK GIN FIZZ

The pink colour in this recipe comes from succulent grenadine rather than an overreliance on anything too edgy or herbaceous, and it tastes fabulous – as fruity and uplifting as cloud-surfing around the world on an inflatable pomegranate. It's a drink I love to sip while relaxing with a favourite movie. From personal experience I can tell you my Pink Gin Fizz makes an excellent pairing with *Guardians of the Galaxy*, but you can of course choose your own favourite. To me, the lurid palate of the first *Guardians* movie along with dynamic characters and easy humour all mirror the epic entertainment that this drink offers. Like all great gatherings, it's hard to pick out a favourite from one of the ingredients because it is, after all, the unique combination that ultimately saves the day. Makes me wonder whether there's scope for a sequel to this drink. Or, just make a second one and call it *Pink Gin Fizz Remastered*.

45ml (1½oz) gin

15ml (½oz) freshly squeezed lime juice

15ml (½oz) freshly squeezed lemon juice

7.5ml (¼oz) grenadine

7.5ml (¼oz) simple syrup (see page 11)

Soda water, to top

Ice: Cubed

Garnish: Lemon and lime wedge

Equipment: Cocktail shaker, strainer

Fill a shaker with ice

Add all the ingredients except the soda water

Shake vigorously to chill

Strain into a glass filled with ice and top with soda water

Garnish with a lemon and lime wedge

TUXEDO #2

Dry vermouth feels like a close cousin to gin, with its aromatic, thirst-quenching potency, and this is further boosted with that dash of absinthe. Remember, absinthe is powerful and pokey, so all that's required is a whisper to echo through the background of this outstanding elixir.

The Tuxedo cocktail recipes all have their simple variations but my favourite and the only one really worth knowing is #2, which is the easiest to remember as it always has equal parts gin and dry vermouth. Stick with simplicity: the Tuxedo has been expanded and complicated over the years, but I reckon #2 comes in first place.

45ml (1½oz) gin

45ml (1½oz) dry vermouth

7.5ml (¼oz) maraschino cherry liqueur

2 dashes Angostura Bitters

Dash orange bitters

Dash absinthe

Ice: Cubed

Garnish: Lemon twist and speared cherry

Equipment: Cocktail shaker, long bar spoon

Fill a shaker with ice

Add all the ingredients except the absinthe

Stir gently to combine

Rinse the inside of a chilled glass with absinthe then discard the excess

Strain the contents of the shaker into the absinthe-rinsed glass

Garnish with a lemon twist and a speared cherry

FLORADORA

Named after an early 1900s musical, this is a really delicious, light pink, refreshing drink that's starting to enjoy a comeback.

The Floradora reminds of Superman: they both come and go in various different guises over the years, and it's high time for the definitive version to step forward and endure. Floradora combines all the stimulation of the very greatest cocktails with a minimum of fuss. And since it's so little known, when you casually knock one up at home it instantly makes you look like a professional bartender with all the knowledge gained from working the world's leading cocktail bar. There is no obligation to wear a tight-fitting Spandex suit while you're making a Floradora, but you could create a secret dance to shuffle your superhero powers from head to toe as you take your first sip.

45ml (1½oz) gin

22.5ml (¾oz) Chambord

15ml (½oz) freshly squeezed lime juice

75ml (2½oz) fiery ginger beer, to top

Ice: Cubed

Garnish: Lime wedge and raspberry

Equipment: Cocktail shaker, strainer

Fill a shaker with ice

Add all the ingredients except the ginger beer

Shake vigorously to chill

Strain into a glass filled with ice and top with the ginger beer

Garnish with a lime wedge and a raspberry

BREAKFAST MARTINI

I've kept the garnish simple here but in some bars they really go to town: I've seen everything from tiny toast wedges to marmalade sandwiches.

The first Breakfast Martini I ever tasted was made by the famous bartender Salvatore Calabrese in St James's in London in a dimly lit memory down a corridor of collected memories on a night out with chef James Martin. An inspiration to cocktail lovers the world over, Maestro Calabrese created me a Breakfast Martini in the middle of the night when, it is entirely possible, if not rather probable, that I was in need of a sustaining sip to refocus my palate and crack right on.

Marmalade is a totally underrated ingredient in cocktails. Not only do you get the flavour, you also get a luxuriant texture – so while Paddington Bear lavishes it on his sandwiches, I much prefer mine in a slick Breakfast Martini.

45ml (1½oz) gin

1 tbsp orange marmalade

22.5ml (¾oz) Cointreau

22.5ml (¾oz) freshly squeezed lemon juice

Ice: Cubed

Garnish: Orange twist

Equipment: Cocktail shaker, strainer, bar spoon

Stir the gin and marmalade together in a shaker until combined

Add the rest of the ingredients along with ice

Shake vigorously to chill

Strain into a chilled glass

Garnish with an orange twist

SINGAPORE SLING

Whenever I glance at the ingredients of the Singapore Sling, I'm always reminded of some of the more inspiringly complex things in life: becoming an astronaut, deep-sea diving and peering from the peak of the Matterhorn. All of them in their own way have their complexities yet all are inherently worth the assembly of equipment and willpower for the adventure ahead – and so is combining all these ingredients. The drink is a classic and there's a reason why it has endured for so many years. It could be whispered in the same breath as Stevie Wonder, Amelia Earhart or the Yeti as an enduring icon. Perhaps the greatest thing of all is that wherever you are in the world, this cocktail comes to you. Sure, you could check in at Singapore's Raffles hotel and experience the cocktail at the Long Bar where, legend has it, the drink was created by bartender Ngiam Tong Boon more than a century ago. But anywhere in the world, you can bring the party to your palate with a bit of ingenuity and my version here, which is lifted by dialling down the grenadine and upping the gin. 'Up the gin' really should be the slogan for the headband we all wear while making this cocktail. I'm designing mine now.

45ml (1½oz) gin

15ml (½oz) cherry brandy

7.5ml (¼oz) Bénédictine

7.5ml (¼oz) grenadine

7.5ml (¼oz) triple sec

120ml (4oz) pineapple juice

15ml (½oz) freshly squeezed lime juice

Ice: Cubed

Garnish: Pineapple wedge and cherry

Equipment: Cocktail shaker, strainer

Fill a shaker with ice

Add all the ingredients

Shake vigorously to chill

Strain into a glass filled with ice

Garnish with a pineapple wedge and a cherry

SOUTHSIDE

Zap! Gin and lemon are both as dazzling as a refreshing bolt of lightning direct to your palate. This cocktail is one of the most invigorating jump-starts to any occasion at home and the trick is all about balancing the freshness of mint with zingy lemon juice.

In terms of skills, all you need is a little bit of focused willpower to deliver this cocktail of clarity and delight. And when you hand one over, stand well back: the effect is often electrifying.

60ml (2oz) gin

30ml (1oz) freshly squeezed lemon juice

15ml (½oz) simple syrup (see page 11)

6–8 mint leaves

Ice: Cubed

Garnish: Mint sprig

Equipment: Cocktail shaker, muddler and strainer

Muddle the mint leaves in the bottom of a shaker then add ice

Add the remaining ingredients

Shake vigorously to chill

Strain into a chilled glass

Garnish with a mint sprig

To make a **Northside** simply swap the gin for vodka.

You can use lime juice instead of lemon juice in both the Southside and Northside.

DISCO
DANCING
MERMAID

I came up with this cocktail one weekend when in search of a drink as azure as a mermaid's eyes. I'd been dreaming of pirates listening to movie soundtracks, you see.

There's something about drinking an azure drink that definitively establishes that you are not at work or somewhere you'd rather not be. In fact, this drink more than any other says: I'm at home and I want to enjoy myself. Partly it's down to the colour.

Blue curaçao manages to turn most things a tropical tinge of sea-blue if you use it in the right quantities, and here I'm topping it off with Champagne, an indulgence you richly deserve. Of course, if you want to save a few pennies you could use crémant, but the flavours of this drink are where it really counts. It's divine, and while it may not turn your eyes quite as azure as a mermaid's, you'll feel just as slinky and magical.

45ml (1½oz) gin

15ml (½oz) blue curaçao

15ml (½oz) freshly squeezed lemon juice

7.5ml (¼oz) simple syrup (see page 11)

Champagne, to top

6 mint leaves

1.5cm (½in) piece of cucumber

Ice: Cubed

Equipment: Shaker, strainer

Muddle the mint leaves and cucumber in a shaker

Fill the shaker with ice and add all the remaining ingredients except the Champagne

Shake vigorously to chill

Double strain into a chilled flute and top with Champagne

TEQUILA

Tequila is a superior spirit. For as long as I can remember it has unfairly been cast as either a party drink or as something simple. In fact the complexity of tequila can be astounding. On a visit to Mexico I was delighted by the range of herby nuances from rosemary to basil that I found in tequila blanco; when the same spirit is aged in oak barrels for between three and 12 months, tequila reposado ('rested'), as it's known, starts to take on a smooth depth I particularly love in cocktails. In a Margarita, for instance, reposado's touch of ageing adds roundness without overpowering. It's what I've used most in these recipes along with blanco. Anything aged for longer is best for sipping neat and revelling in the complexity.

When selecting tequila, it pays to know about the terms that feature on labels. Tequila has to be made from a minimum of 51% agave (a spiky plant native to the Americas), with the rest of the liquid prior to distillation coming from corn or cane sugars, known in the trade as 'mixto'. If you see '100% agave' on a label, that tequila has been made solely from the agave plant, and it's what I tend to buy and use most often for my cocktails – in my view 100% agave delivers some of the very best flavours.

It takes many years – sometimes a decade or more – to grow the succulent, structural leaves of Agave tequilana, or blue agave. Blue agave thrives in the Mexican heat and is harvested and trimmed by *jimadors* for the heart or piña, which is then cooked and crushed traditionally by a stone press known as a *tahona* (often pulled by oxen, mules or donkeys). The resulting pulp is fermented and distilled at least twice into the magic elixir – but to be officially classified as tequila, the spirit must be based on blue agave from one of five Mexican states, the most prominent being Jalisco.

Probably the most widely known tequila category is **Blanco** (which you may have heard described as 'silver', a term coined by the José Cuervo brand). This is tequila at its purest and while it can be aged in oak for no more than 60 days, more often than not it's settled in stainless steel to keep that bright clarity.

Joven is a blend of tequila blanco and aged tequila. Avoid joven that's been tinted to a gold colour by adding caramel – instead I'd recommend closely scrutinising the bottle's label for some evidence of aged tequilas, or go for a clearly labelled reposado instead.

Reposado, which I love to use in cocktails, is aged in oak for more than 60 days. Again, avoid any with caramel, as you won't get the same depth of flavour as you do with wood ageing. The size of the oak vessels used varies and may be charred or have previously contained other spirits such as American whiskey, so the impact of oak ageing can be massive. Whether it's from a smaller cask or a large vat (known as a *pipote*), it really pays to taste a few different reposados to settle on your favourite.

Añejo is aged for more than one year in an oak vessel with a maximum capacity of 60 litres. Again, check the label for added caramel.

Extra añejo is similar to añejo but must be aged for more than three years. I'd sip añejo and extra añejo to enjoy their inherent complexity rather than blend them into cocktails. Your call, of course. My tip is to stick to reposado or blanco for the base of these recipes and embrace tequila's naturally upbeat capacity for creating good times and great flavours at home.

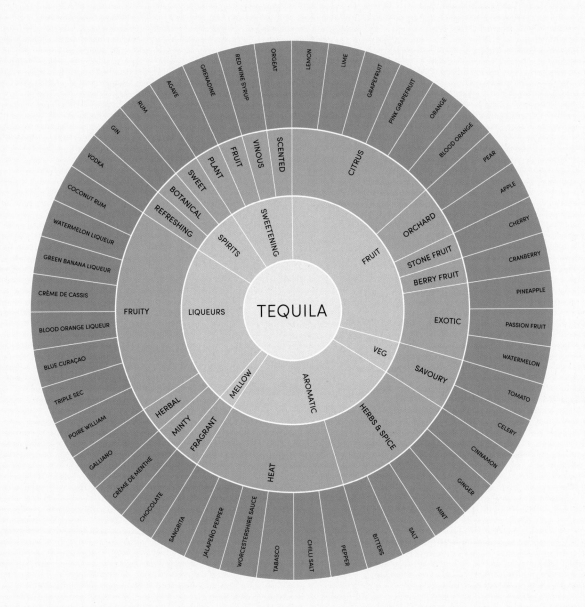

FREDDY FUDPUCKER

This memorably named variation of the Harvey Wallbanger switches out vodka for tequila. The fresh orange juice makes all the difference and is so worthwhile. Just that little bit of elbow work can bring bar quality to your home. The effect of using tequila makes the drink a little richer and more flavoursome: perfect for sipping after dinner. You could almost describe the Fudpucker as a Harvey Wallbanger where, thanks to tequila reposado, the wall has been made with bricks of gold. Follow the yellow brick wall!

60ml (2oz) tequila reposado

120ml (4oz) freshly squeezed orange juice

15ml (½oz) Galliano

Ice: Cubed

Garnish: Orange-cherry sail

Equipment: Cocktail shaker, strainer

Fill a shaker with ice

Add all the ingredients except the Galliano

Shake vigorously to chill

Strain into a glass filled with ice

Garnish with an orange-cherry sail

Float the Galliano on top with the back of a teaspoon

MARGARITA -
STRAIGHT UP

The thought of making Margaritas takes me straight to celebrating my wife Sophie's twenty-first birthday some years ago. Her uncle Felix – a man so hearty he always looks as though he's just summited Ben Nevis – made pitchers of the stuff and got everybody surfing waves of joy from the edges of his salty-rimmed concoctions. In my recipe, the salt rim enhances the flavour in the triple sec to magical effect. And you can customise as you please – a chilli salt rim to spice things up is another great option. I love the Margarita because it does justice to the complexity of tequila while emphasising its core character of refreshment. I adore the nuanced herbal flavours tequila can carry – think rosemary – and the Margarita manages to guard that subtlety while simultaneously unleashing the full spectrum of its main constituent's zing. It's basically a citrus sabre of a drink – it cuts through everything, and the thrill of this particular recipe is the spirited feeling of freshness enhanced with depth and texture from the triple sec and agave syrup. It's a glorious drink to serve in a coupe glass for a simple sense of occasion and just as appropriate at a party as it is late morning for a weekend pick-me-up. Perhaps it might even inspire you to hop up a mountain, metaphorical or otherwise, rather like the Margarita's biggest fan of all, Uncle Felix.

45ml (1½oz) tequila reposado

15ml (½oz) triple sec

30ml (1oz) freshly squeezed lime juice

15ml (½oz) agave syrup

Ice: Cubed

Garnish: Salt rim and lime wedge

Equipment: Cocktail shaker, strainer

Rim a chilled glass with salt

Fill a shaker with ice

Add all the ingredients

Shake vigorously to chill

Strain into the salt-rimmed glass

Garnish with a lime wedge

MARGARITA –
FROZEN

The most inspiring frozen Margarita I've tasted was a while ago in Edinburgh's El Cartel – a tiny little joint on Thistle Street in the New Town. It was silky-smooth and dispatched me into a delighted reverie about savoury sorbet which lasted for hours. As well as the classic frozen Margarita, the flavoured varieties are also sublime. You can try this at home – it is so simple, just add 60ml (2oz) of your favourite fruit purée to the recipe. Kapow!

The freezing takes the mighty Margarita to the next level. It's a jolt of invigoration as bracing as diving from a cloud of hot steam into the heart of an iceberg. For a summer drink, nothing beats the frozen Margarita to cool down outdoors. And in between courses as a palate cleanser, it's guaranteed to get the party started. To avoid the drink loosening into slush, remember my rule of thumb: drink your frozen Margarita like you're skiing to a party – fast and cold.

45ml (1½oz) tequila reposado

15ml (½oz) triple sec (or you can use Grand Marnier if you don't have triple sec)

30ml (1oz) freshly squeezed lime juice

15ml (½oz) agave syrup

Ice: Crushed

Garnish: Salt rim and lime wedge

Equipment: Blender

Rim a chilled glass with salt

Place 1 scoop of crushed ice into a blender cup

Add all the ingredients

Blend until smooth

Pour into a hurricane glass

Garnish with a lime wedge

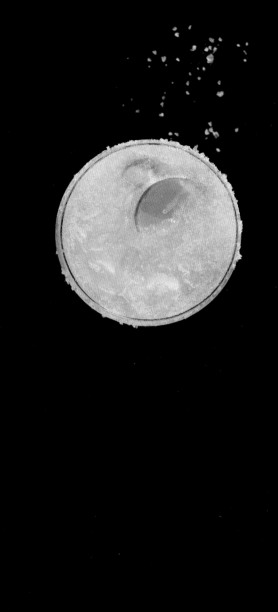

PALOMA

Paloma means 'dove' in Spanish, and this version of the cocktail got me thinking of the pink legs on the white doves that delighted me while I was spending some time in Seville. They gracefully curled around the 16th-century cathedral with a flash of their colourful feet as they stretched to perch. There was a moment in particular that stands out. I was on a rooftop one afternoon sipping a simple version of the Paloma (tequila and pink grapefruit juice with heaps of frosty ice). I distinctly remember Halley's Comet searing and blazing steadily in the hot haze above. I felt quenched and cool as the glowing comet held me in its spell. That moment of marvel inspired this recipe – a citrus sparkler of a long drink that invigorates and inspires inward and outward contemplation. You can sip it quietly or pour a couple for a conversational safari, and it's the perfect cocktail to rev up your appetite when there's spicy food on the menu. For a real one-off, try it with fish and chips – it transforms the chippy's best into a winner of a dinner.

60ml (2oz) tequila reposado

22.5ml (¾oz) pink grapefruit juice

15ml (½oz) freshly squeezed lime juice

7.5ml (¼oz) agave syrup

Grapefruit soda, to top

Ice: Cubed

Garnish: Grapefruit slice and lime wheel

Equipment: Cocktail shaker, strainer

Fill a shaker with ice

Add all the ingredients except the grapefruit soda

Shake vigorously to chill

Strain into a glass filled with ice

Top with grapefruit soda

Garnish with quarter of a grapefruit slice and a lime wheel

TEQUILA SUNRISE

This cocktail was created by bartender Bobby Lozoff, who famously made it for Mick Jagger at the Trident in Sausalito, California, to kick off the Rolling Stones' US tour in 1972. Jagger loved it so much he made it throughout the tour (which was informally dubbed 'the cocaine and Tequila Sunrise tour' by the band) and the cocktail's fame kicked off like a backstage party gatecrashed by a rhino on gold-sequinned rollerskates.

If you find this recipe on the sweet side, just add a dash of lime juice to sharpen things into focus. Talking of focus, the movie *Tequila Sunrise* opened in cinemas in 1988 with Mel Gibson, Michelle Pfeiffer and Kurt Russell, a crime drama set in a seaside Californian town with best friends on opposite sides of the law. The gradation of deep glowing red at the base to bright orange at the top of the drink is similar to the blurred lines of the movie – two friends split by the love of the same woman – ultimately blending into a seamless tale of adventure and intrigue. The drink stands alone as an icon, and although 'sunrise' does feature in the name, I'm not advocating that you leap out of bed and drink this cocktail in the shower. It is, however, a great drink for late mornings on a day off or when on holiday because it slips down so easily. You could drift into dreaming of Californian high jinks without even stepping out of your front door.

45ml (1½oz) tequila reposado

120ml (4oz) freshly squeezed orange juice

15ml (½oz) grenadine

Ice: Cubed

Garnish: Orange slice and cherry

Equipment: Long bar spoon

Fill a glass with ice

Add the tequila and orange juice

Stir to combine

Pour the grenadine down the inside edge of the glass: it will drop through the drink, giving a sunrise effect

Garnish with an orange slice and cherry

SUNBURN

I remember a few years ago roaming rural Sicily seeking out little-known vineyards with grapes wonderful enough to blend into a wine I was creating for the UK market. Vino aside, there were two highlights of the trip. Firstly, the ruins of the ancient Greek temples at Valle dei Templi, which has been a Unesco World Heritage Site since 1997. And secondly, the blood oranges growing near Mount Etna, which were abundant on my springtime visit. The intensity of my Sunburn cocktail flows from the unique character of blood orange juice – deeper, richer, more exotic and with a thrilling edge to the flavour that feels like peel from a red pencil sharpener. That breathtaking tartness is as similarly immediate as a slap on a sunburnt back, yet the genius of this recipe is the assuaging balm of its instant cool refreshment. And while I prize the Sicilian blood oranges just as highly as the magnificence of venerable temples of antiquity, it's fine to use freshly squeezed standard orange juice if you can't get hold of them. Just make sure you raise your glass to the red gold of Sicily and the beauty of the blood orange.

45ml (1½oz) tequila reposado

15ml (½oz) triple sec

60ml (2oz) freshly squeezed blood orange juice

60ml (2oz) cranberry juice

Ice: Cubed

Garnish: Blood orange slice

Equipment: Long bar spoon

Fill a glass with ice

Add all the ingredients

Stir gently to combine

Garnish with a slice of blood orange

EL DIABLO

A historic cocktail whose origins are as shrouded in mystery as the devil himself. Iconic stuff from the vault of tequila's titillation, this drink is as red as the devil's horns and the fiery ginger beer gives it wicked spice. Rather like Lucifer, this cocktail is great fun to hang out with and far more entertaining than the good guys. Straightforward to master, El Diablo flows from temptation's very fount. Why would you even try to resist?

45ml (1½oz) tequila reposado

15ml (½oz) crème de cassis

15ml (½oz) freshly squeezed lime juice

75ml (2½oz) fiery ginger beer, to top

Ice: Crushed

Garnish: Lime wedge

Equipment: Long bar spoon

Fill a glass two-thirds with crushed ice

Add all the ingredients except the ginger beer

Stir gently to combine

Top with the ginger beer and cap with more crushed ice

Garnish with a lime wedge

CHIMAYO

A gorgeous, subtle lavender tint evolves in this drink, and the summer fruit conveys holiday heaven. Chimayo is in north-central New Mexico, and the story goes that the original recipe was engineered to soak up a surplus of apples. It's certainly a favourite in the region, especially around autumn when the orchard fruits are falling – it's a lovely cocktail to reflect on the bounty of a beneficent harvest. Here's to the good things that grow and to the flavours that drift through this delicious drink.

45ml (1½oz) tequila reposado

7.5ml (¼oz) crème de cassis

90ml (3oz) cloudy apple juice

15ml (½oz) freshly squeezed lemon juice

7.5ml (¼oz) agave syrup

Ice: Cubed

Garnish: Apple slices

Equipment: Cocktail shaker, strainer

Fill a shaker with ice

Add all the ingredients

Shake vigorously to chill

Strain into a glass filled with ice

Garnish with slices of apple

MEXICAN SURFER

The Mexican Surfer epitomises what a great cocktail should be: easy to create, and expands on a quality spirit with simple ingredients. I'd add to that the ice-cold element ensures a wonderfully refreshing experience, just like catching a wave in the Mexican sunshine. I am fortunate to have surfed a few waves in Mexico (as well as where I grew up, on the island of Jersey, learning how to boogie board). I was never proficient enough to stand up and actually surf, so with this drink in my hand I salute the big-wave surfers of the world whose feats are jaw-dropping. And just as a surfer loves the ocean, pineapple and tequila fulfil one another's potential. The acidity and texture of pineapple boosted with lime cordial... well, it just feels like you're at the crest of tequila's tastiest wave! Ride it today. And know that this is a wave without end.

60ml (2oz) tequila reposado

45ml (1½oz) pineapple juice

15ml (½oz) lime cordial

Ice: Cubed

Garnish: Lime twist

Equipment: Cocktail shaker, strainer

Fill a shaker with ice

Add all the ingredients

Shake vigorously to chill

Strain into a chilled glass

Garnish with a lime twist

You can swap out the lime cordial for 60ml (2oz) coconut rum.

TEQUILA MOCKINGBIRD

Although it's divinely green, this cocktail – name aside – has nothing to do with Harper Lee's *To Kill A Mockingbird*. However, it's still one of the most quotable names in the cocktail hall of fame. Interestingly, there is an extraordinarily diverse range of recipes and colours for this cocktail. I took my inspiration from crème de menthe, the secret potion I used to sip to invoke grammatical gymnastics during my years studying for my English degree. Crème de menthe was in its wilderness years in the 1990s, but it always reminded me of David Bowie – forever intriguing and never far from the edge of inspiration. Crème de menthe has probably been hiding at the back of your drinks cabinet like a forgotten love letter, and it's high time you dived back in. Just as old words string Cupid's bow, these ingredients come together to deliver a gripping dart of intrigue. Like a romantic page-turner, you just can't put this classic down.

60ml (2oz) tequila reposado

15ml (½oz) crème de menthe

15ml (½oz) freshly squeezed lime juice

7.5ml (¼oz) agave syrup

Ice: Cubed

Garnish: Mint sprig

Equipment: Cocktail shaker, strainer

Fill a shaker with ice

Add all the ingredients

Shake vigorously to chill

Strain into a chilled glass

Garnish with a mint sprig

MEXICAN FIRING SQUAD

Charles H. Baker Jr's 1939 book *The Gentleman's Companion* brought this drink legions of fresh fans. It was named after a notorious session in Mexico City's La Cucaracha Cocktail Club a couple of years earlier, when travelling man Charles and his buddies indulged in a cohort of these drinks. My version sticks to the classic high-impact origins with grenadine rounding things out with its mellow, exotic sweetness.

For some reason this cocktail, which is almost a century old, has been overlooked for all these years – really baffling when you think about it. Surely a drink born of a great night out in Mexico belongs at the centre of every great night in at home! While one of these may give you the urge to dance, a few are almost certain to end up starting a kitchen fiesta.

60ml (2oz) tequila reposado

22.5ml (¾oz) freshly squeezed lime juice

15ml (½oz) grenadine

2 dashes bitters

Ice: Cubed

Garnish: Lime wedge

Equipment: Cocktail shaker, strainer

Fill a shaker with ice

Add all the ingredients

Shake vigorously to chill

Strain into a glass filled with ice

Garnish with a lime wedge

To make a more modern, longer drink simply serve in a tall Collins glass and top with soda.

POIRE
BOUDOIR

This drink is the place where pear shows its true splendour. I'm baffled that pears don't feature more often in cocktails – why should this singular fruit be so hush-hush? Time to unlock the poire boudoir and invite the world to revel in the mysteriously mellow yet tingling freshness. The light, fruity fragrance links sublimely with the scented, herbaceous character of tequila. This underrated concoction is elevated in the poire boudoir by lime juice, and the rich, sweet strata of grenadine discreetly closes the door behind you as you tumble into the realm of pleasure. The first person who bravely stepped into the Poire Boudoir was Dave Lamb, the voice of *Come Dine With Me*. He's been a willing test pilot for a number of my cocktail creations over the years, and his response to this was memorable: 'Peary good.' I'll take that.

45ml (1½oz) tequila reposado

15ml (½oz) Poire Williams

45ml (1½oz) pear juice

7.5ml (¼oz) freshly squeezed lime juice

Dash grenadine

Ice: Cubed

Garnish: Fanned pear

Equipment: Cocktail shaker, strainer

Fill a shaker with ice

Add all the ingredients

Shake vigorously to chill

Strain into chilled glass

Garnish with a fanned pear

If you want something a little smokier try mezcal instead of the tequila.

SILK STOCKING

The watchwords here are silky and smooth –
this is a cocktail to unwind with, the balm after
a hectic day. It's also a sleeper of a classic and
when you first make it for your friends, they'll
be as impressed and unexpectedly delighted
as they would be on a spontaneous night in
with the voice of Dolly Parton and the spirit of
Prince as your house guests.

60ml (2oz) tequila blanco

22.5ml (¾oz) white crème de cacao

22.5ml (¾oz) single (light) cream

7.5ml (¼oz) grenadine

Ice: Cubed

Garnish: Chocolate and cinnamon powders

Equipment: Cocktail shaker, strainer

Fill a shaker with ice

Add all the ingredients

Shake vigorously to chill

Strain into a chilled glass

Garnish with a sprinkle of chocolate and
cinnamon powders

If you don't have tequila blanco then reposado is
a decent substitute. I do prefer the lighter touch
of blanco (unoaked), though, as it helps keep this
drink curiously light.

BLOODY MARIA

Fire up the spice engines and three, two, one, IGNITION! This riff on the Bloody Mary is a liquid firecracker. The red wine syrup adds a depth and richness which combines with the sharp spiciness of the Sangrita, a heady blend with a kick that could rouse Sleeping Beauty from fifty paces. The agave plant behind tequila matches sublimely with savoury flavours and takes on the fiery twist in this cocktail, neatly complementing its punchy character. Is there ever a better moment than now for a Bloody Maria? It's a 24/7 recipe, all year round – and, of course, having one at brunch is a no-brainer. I urge you to find the touchpaper in your mind, strike the match of your intention and soar into the stratosphere with a Bloody Maria powering you into an orbit of ease.

45ml (1½oz) tequila reposado

120ml (4oz) Sangrita (see page 128)

15ml (½oz) red wine syrup (see page 11)

Ice: Cubed

Garnish: Jalapeño pepper

Equipment: Long bar spoon

Fill a glass with ice

Add all the ingredients

Stir gently to combine

Garnish with half a jalapeño pepper

Don't nibble the garnish on this one. It's there to add heat and colour!

SANGRITA

This is the traditional way to enjoy a really good tequila. The recipe makes a half-litre batch that can be used in Bloody Marias (page 126) as well as for a tequila chaser.

Sangrita recipes are hugely varied and there's no right or wrong way of making one. Have fun creating a version to your taste. As a guide, this is a lot thinner than a traditional Bloody Mary mix. If you like it sweeter you can add 15ml (½oz) grenadine.

This recipe is like your favourite jumper – it never lets you down and it pays to take it wherever you go. It's a phenomenal tribute to umami's dalliance with all the other flavours – sharp twists, richness, spice and zing. The secret to the Sangrita's success is the tension it carries, like a trampoline of taste to ping you into the next dimension of deliciousness. As a chaser, the Sangrita highlights the refreshing side of tequila and simultaneously gets you ready for the next sip. It's a wonderful drink to get the party travelling thirst class in the minimum space of time. You should deploy it today – think of it like a virtuous cattle prod for your mood that'll give you an electrifying sense of invigoration. Take the leap.

300ml (10½oz) tomato juice

100ml (3½oz) grapefruit juice

100ml (3½oz) orange juice

1 jalapeño pepper, including seeds, halved

Large dash Worcestershire sauce

Large dash Tabasco

1 tsp celery salt

Pinch salt and pepper

Equipment: Long bar spoon

Combine all the ingredients in a large jug along with the halved jalapeño pepper

Chill in the fridge

Remove the chilli after an hour or so, depending on how hot you want it to be

Serve in a chilled shot glass alongside your favourite sipping tequila

ADIOS MF

As the name suggests, this drink is not the height of sophistication, but it tastes great and is the perfect party drink. Lemon-lime soda can be anything along the lines of Sprite or 7 Up.

Adios MF is as cocky and confident as its name. For me, it's always a party drink and takes me back to long nights in San Diego with my friend Handsome Jim (think Bradley Cooper meets Tom Hiddleston). Jim is the master of whipping up an Adios MF with the grace of a stallion and the power of a bear. If you like a Long Island Iced Tea you'll love this recipe, and since blue drinks are always fun in a slightly outrageous way, you could certainly say this cocktail reflects the naughtiness of its name... although strangely I always feel virtuous after making the effort to put it together. I guess it's a drink of contradictions, the biggest one being that in spite of its multiple ingredients, it's a singular star of balance in cocktail creativity. And if you make enough of it, you might even lure Handsome Jim himself to share one with you.

15ml (½oz) tequila reposado

15ml (½oz) white rum

15ml (½oz) vodka

15ml (½oz) gin

15ml (½oz) blue curaçao

30ml (1oz) freshly squeezed lemon juice

15ml (½oz) simple syrup (see page 11)

30ml (1oz) lemon-lime soda, to top

Ice: Cubed

Garnish: Lemon-cherry sail

Equipment: Cocktail shaker, strainer

Fill a shaker with ice

Add all the ingredients except the lemon-lime soda

Shake vigorously to chill

Strain into a glass filled with ice and top with the lemon-lime soda

Garnish with a lemon-cherry sail

MANZANA PASSION

I know, green banana liqueur may not be top of your list of things to rush out and buy for your cocktail shelf. Thing is, it's delicious. The green colour is a bit of fun but the flavour is the serious bit – it's less sweet than a traditional banana liqueur, which in the case of the Manzana Passion blends seamlessly with the sharpness of both passion fruit and apple. It's that central fruity duo that duets in a dance of deliciousness around the central pillar of tequila, and it's all lifted up by lime juice's edgy zip. The taste is exquisite, but the structure of this sumptuous drink is so spellbinding it'll turn your thoughts to dreams.

45ml (1½oz) tequila reposado

15ml (½oz) green banana liqueur

75ml (2½oz) cloudy apple juice

15ml (½oz) freshly squeezed lime juice

15ml (½oz) passion fruit purée

Ice: Cubed

Garnish: Apple slice and lime wedge

Equipment: Cocktail shaker, muddler and strainer

Fill a shaker with ice

Add all the ingredients

Shake vigorously to chill

Strain into a glass filled with ice

Garnish with an apple slice and lime wedge

FUEGO WATERMELON

One of a select few cocktails that pulls off the magic trick of being spicy, salty and fruity all at once. I'm taking the soul of a Watermelon Margarita and firing it from a bazooka into the bullseye of inspiration. I love drinking my Fuego Watermelons with spicy and zesty nibbles as partners to the cooling watermelon effect. Anyone for Bombay Mix?

45ml (1½oz) tequila reposado

15ml (½oz) watermelon liqueur

15ml (½oz) freshly squeezed lime juice

7.5ml (¼oz) chilli simple syrup (see page 11)

15ml (½oz) orange juice

30g (1oz) fresh watermelon (or the same amount of purée)

Ice: Crushed

Garnish: Watermelon slice and chilli salt rim

Equipment: Blender

Rim a glass with chilli salt

Add a scoop of crushed ice to a blender cup

Add all the ingredients

Blend until smooth

Tap into the glass, being careful not to disturb the chilli salt rim

Garnish with a slice of watermelon

TIKI TEQUILA

Exotic Pacific island tiki bars were all the rage in the 50s and 60s in the USA. There was a revival in the 1990s and they continue to come and go. The best one I ever visited was an underground establishment in Lewes, East Sussex, that went by the codename 'Puddings'. With a lifesize cutout of Tom Selleck behind the bar sporting a rampant red Hawaiian shirt, Puddings was the hottest tiki ticket for cocktails and popped up in unexpected places when you least expected it. Selleck aside, I have always loved the tiki mugs, tropical decor and volcano-on-sea appeal of these bars. And it pays to stick to the tropical theme – the tiki bar I once set up at home looked as though an ostrich had exploded at the entrance to a goldmine: way too much glitter and feathers everywhere. To save you the trouble of building a bar, this is the drink you'll need to make any night of the week feel like tiki time. Thanks to the orgeat and pineapple in particular, my Tiki Tequila is a shortcut to feeling instantly exotic – step through the portal to paradise. And remember to raise your glass to Puddings.

45ml (1½oz) tequila reposado

15ml (½oz) blood orange liqueur

15ml (½oz) freshly squeezed lime juice

15ml (½oz) pineapple juice

7.5ml (¼oz) orgeat

7.5ml (¼oz) agave syrup

Ice: Cubed

Garnish: Dehydrated orange slice

Equipment: Cocktail shaker, strainer

Fill a shaker with ice

Add all the ingredients

Shake vigorously to chill

Strain into a glass filled with ice

Garnish with a dehydrated orange slice

LAGERITA

Who doesn't like mixing beer into cocktails?! I first got a taste for it in Los Angeles, when the sheer heat of the day drove me into the shade of a cool Santa Monica beach bar where everyone was drinking Lageritas. These are a longer version of the Margarita, topped with ice-cold Mexican beer. Mexican beer tends to be light, bright and – in a good way – not too heavy on flavour, which is beautifully refreshing on a hot day. And agave syrup gives the drink a subtle boost of mellow richness. Remember, tequila is made from agave, so these two are closely related and always work well together in cocktails. When you've got a Lagerita in your hand, all you need is an imaginary sun hat to make you feel like you're relaxing beachside.

45ml (1½oz) tequila reposado

15ml (½oz) triple sec

22.5ml (¾oz) freshly squeezed lime juice

7.5ml (¼oz) agave syrup

90ml (3oz) Mexican beer, to top

Ice: Cubed

Garnish: Lime wheel

Equipment: Cocktail shaker, muddler and strainer

Fill a shaker with ice

Add all the ingredients except the beer

Shake vigorously to chill

Strain into a glass filled with ice

Top with beer

Garnish with a lime wheel

TEQUILA
FIZZ

All things that sparkle are splendid: sequins, diamonds, fireworks. And bubbles. This is as bright and invigorating as light reflecting off the sea beneath a midday sun. Great for parties, fantastic for transforming a moment into a special occasion, it lifts the tequila and pays homage to its intrinsic bright side. This is a cocktail that always supplies a glass half-full vibe: it's a mood-raising collection of zesty ingredients that takes any moment from slump to stratosphere.

60ml (2oz) tequila reposado

30ml (1oz) freshly squeezed orange juice

30ml (1oz) freshly squeezed lime juice

15ml (½oz) agave syrup

45ml (1½oz) grapefruit soda, to top

Ice: Cubed

Garnish: Orange twist

Equipment: Cocktail shaker, strainer

Fill a shaker with ice

Add all the ingredients except the grapefruit soda

Shake vigorously to chill

Strain into a glass filled with ice

Top with grapefruit soda and garnish with an orange twist

TEQUILA SMASH

A cousin of the Brandy Smash, the Tequila Smash is dependent on gently muddling the mint to release its aromatic invigoration. No need to pound it, just gently apply pressure and enjoy the scent as it slowly fills the space around you. Really simple to make, this cocktail massively overdelivers on enjoyment. It offers a compact, classy drink that manages to be as intense as it is enticing. My most memorable Tequila Smash was in Barcelona in a dodgy dockside bar when I saw The Darkness playing a tiny gig before their fame went through the roof. My day was made when the band hailed the cab I was in to nip into town for some dinner. As I sipped my Tequila Smash I raised it to the band and gave it a codename in their honour: Love on the Rocks.

60ml (2oz) tequila reposado

7.5ml (¼oz) agave syrup

15ml (½oz) freshly squeezed lemon juice

6–8 mint leaves

Ice: Cubed

Garnish: Mint sprig

Equipment: Cocktail shaker, muddler and strainer

Muddle the mint leaves in a shaker

Fill the shaker with ice and add the remaining ingredients

Shake vigorously to chill

Strain into a glass filled with ice

Garnish with a mint sprig

You can try muddling different herbs or fruits to make your own smash creation.

BRANDY

Aside from being a terrific word to bellow like a happy hurricane addressing the wide skies of an endless party, brandy is probably best known for being the festive season's favourite spirit. Father Christmas himself is a fan – in my home, Rudolph's carrot is chomped to the root every year and dear Santa knocks back a dose of the good stuff. I'm pretty sure he once helped himself to the bottle before continuing his rounds. Glad to think it hit the spot. Brandy's warming character can be wonderful in the winter months, although I reckon an overlooked virtue is its versatility in cocktails. It blends brilliantly with everything from cream and chocolate to orange and lemon. For me, it's always been a drink for every season and creates some of the most scrumptious cocktails of all.

Wine regions often produce brandy from grapes. You could almost say that it's wine taken to the next dimension. Armagnac and Cognac, both in France, are the two most famous regions and are known for their careful oak-barrel ageing. While Armagnac tends to be the province of smaller producers and is historically enjoyed by a domestic market, Cognac's closer proximity to major ports enabled it to grow global appreciation for its brands. As far as cocktails go, a youthful Cognac is my top choice to blend and is perfect for wherever you see 'brandy' in these recipes. My rule of thumb is to pick a VSOP – 'Very Superior Old Pale' – a phrase which according to legend was coined by King George IV of the United Kingdom when ordering some top-notch brandy to get stuck into. In a VSOP the youngest part of the blend must be aged for at least four years in barrel, although the blender

may choose older spirits as well. The gentle, spicy character of the wood that VSOP Cognac has been aged in gives a wonderful, fruity balance which, for cocktails, is a playful crossroads leading to sharp, sweet, creamy or aromatic, depending on what you fancy.

And in this chapter I also include grappa from Italy, which is made from grape pomace, as well as pisco from Peru and Chile, which is distilled from fermented grape juice. I love pisco so much that I bought the domain name piscodisco.com – although I still haven't quite fathomed what the website would be for. Perhaps I am destined to one day open a disco that only serves pisco. Fancy coming along?

I've also put Calvados in this chapter, which is French apple brandy from Normandy. It's highly underrated stuff with more than 200 varieties. Just like Cognac, Calvados must be double distilled before it's aged in oak casks. If you're ever at a loose end, driving through the orchards of Normandy's Pays d'Auge with the orchards rippling pink with springtime blossom is a scent worth a thousand roses.

You'll also find I've included apricot brandy – more often than not this is a liqueur laced with fruit rather than a spirit distilled from apricots, although such bottles of liquid fire can be found. You're fine sticking to standard apricot brandy for rounding out these cocktail recipes – I'd suggest saving the proper stuff for enjoying neat.

Let's bellow our love for brandy and start sipping this beautiful spirit in style.

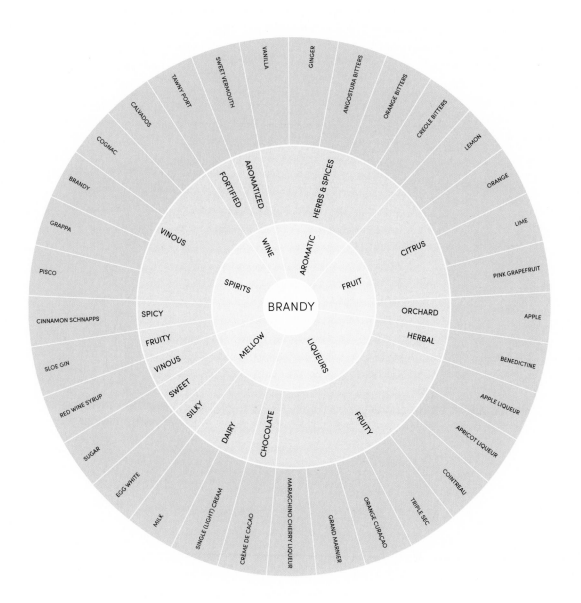

PISCO SOUR
AKA PISCO DISCO

I drank Pisco Sours with relentless enthusiasm throughout my stay in Chile while filming a wine documentary over many months. Pisco, generally made of grapes distilled in the north of the country as well as in neighbouring Peru, has a beautiful fragrance, and with the egg white it's astonishing how refreshing this drink is. And since you're going to the effort of making one, I strongly suggest a second to follow with impeccable timing. A hidden gem for too long, pisco is a beautiful South American brandy and makes a perfect summer drink to sip in the shade.

60ml (2oz) pisco

30ml (1oz) freshly squeezed lemon juice

15ml (½oz) simple syrup (see page 11)

½ an egg white

Ice: Cubed

Garnish: Three drops of bitters

Equipment: Cocktail shaker, strainer

Add all the ingredients to a shaker and shake without ice

Add ice to the shaker and shake until the mixture is chilled

Strain into a chilled glass

Garnish with 3 drops of bitters on the top of the drink

Feel free to swap out the pisco for grappa: whichever is to hand will work just fine.

CORPSE REVIVER #1

Reputed to be a very potent hangover cure.

My Corpse Reviver is a trilogy of temptation that's epic in its impact. Cognac, Calvados and aromatic vermouth unite like the best backing band to the lead singer of your big night in. And this drink is their greatest hit – my Corpse Reviver is ready to kick things off (or close proceedings). Like all classics, it's the little details that stick in the mind, and the orange twist is well worth the effort here. While I cannot guarantee this drink will revive you, I can say with certainty that it's headline entertainment.

45ml (1½oz) brandy (ideally VSOP Cognac)

22.5ml (¾oz) Calvados

22.5ml (¾oz) sweet vermouth

Ice: Cubed

Garnish: Orange twist

Equipment: Cocktail shaker, strainer, long bar spoon

Fill a shaker with ice

Add all the ingredients

Stir gently to combine

Strain into a chilled glass

Zest and garnish with an orange twist

FROUPE

Froupe is the perfect name for a cantankerous poodle. It is also one of the simplest and most delicious cocktails in this book. Bénédictine, the sacred hooch of holiness, is blended with the outrageousness of sweet vermouth's aromatic flair.

Survey it in silence as though in prayer before you drink then crack on with my blessing as you reflect on the devotion of all the work and time that goes into this great liqueur. Famous in the 1930s but now oft-forgotten, this boozy, bittersweet gem is the nightcap of your dreams.

45ml (1½oz) brandy

45ml (1½oz) sweet vermouth

7.5ml (¼oz) Bénédictine

Ice: Cubed

Garnish: Orange twist

Equipment: Long bar spoon

Fill a shaker with ice

Add all the ingredients

Stir gently to combine

Strain into a chilled glass

Garnish with an orange twist

SIDECAR

The Sidecar is a classic cocktail that romped across the world in the early 20th century. For some reason it makes me think of mobsters, sharp suits, tommy guns and the endless roar of an eternal speakeasy. It's one of my favourite brandy cocktails and invokes an era where, if asked how you're doing, the answer is always 'Swell.' Brandy's oak ageing is amplified by the Cointreau – like a referee's alternative whistle blowing to let you know it's never half time on this drink and full time doesn't exist.

45ml (1½oz) brandy

22.5ml (¾oz) Cointreau

22.5ml (¾oz) freshly squeezed lemon juice

Ice: Cubed

Garnish: Lemon twist and sugar rim

Equipment: Cocktail shaker, strainer

Fill a shaker with ice

Add all the ingredients

Shake vigorously to chill

Pour into a chilled glass that has been rimmed with sugar

Garnish with a lemon twist

The sugar rim is optional but as this is quite a dry drink it adds a little hint of sweetness.

BRANDY ALEX

Perhaps it's this cocktail over all others that shows how beautifully brandy pairs with creamy and chocolate flavours. It's rich and velvety and perfect for a frosty time of year or as an after-dinner indulgence: as deluxe as it is delicious. As an all-year-rounder, I love it served instead of a dessert or for a teatime treat.

45ml (1½oz) brandy

30ml (1oz) dark crème de cacao

30ml (1oz) single (light) cream

Ice: Cubed

Garnish: Grated nutmeg

Equipment: Cocktail shaker, strainer

Fill a shaker with ice

Add all the ingredients

Shake vigorously to chill

Strain into a chilled glass

Garnish with a light dusting of grated nutmeg

Swap out the brandy for gin to make an **Alexander**, the lesser-known but original version of a Brandy Alex. The brandy version dates from the 1930s and has held centre stage ever since.

BRANDY CRUSTA

The Brandy Crusta summarises summertime in the warmest climes. A place where orange groves fringe cherry trees, and lemons bulge within sight of sugar cane, exotic herbs, trees and spices. This is a portable passport to that imaginary land where the sun never sets.

With a place assured in the classic cocktail pantheon, the Brandy Crusta's heritage stretches back to the mid-1800s in New Orleans, where it was named after its crusted rim of sugar. It's as enthralling as discovering the world's most comfortable air bed on a shore so tranquil it could be mistaken for a painting: set up your easel and draw some colour into your day with this classic drop of brandy brilliance.

52.5ml (1¾oz) brandy

7.5ml (¼oz) orange curaçao

7.5ml (¼oz) maraschino cherry liqueur

15ml (½oz) freshly squeezed lemon juice

7.5ml (¼oz) simple syrup (see page 11)

2 dashes Angostura Bitters

Ice: Cubed

Garnish: Sugar rim and lemon twist

Equipment: Cocktail shaker, strainer

Fill a shaker with ice

Add all the ingredients

Shake vigorously to chill

Strain into a chilled sugar-rimmed glass

Garnish with an extra-long lemon twist pushed down under the sugar rim

You can swap out the brandy for pisco.

BRANDY SANAGREE

I love tawny port because it tastes like a merry band of flaming sultanas performing gymnastics across your taste buds. Deepened by brandy's heartiness and sweetened with simple syrup, this is a surprisingly delicious drink to sharpen your appetite before lunch (it also makes a divine digestif). If this was in one of those adverts with a before and after photo, they would both look the same: your grinning face, aglow with wonder.

60ml (2oz) brandy

30ml (1oz) tawny port

7.5ml (¼oz) simple syrup (see page 11)

Ice: Cubed

Garnish: Grated nutmeg

Equipment: Cocktail shaker, strainer, long bar spoon

Fill a shaker with ice

Add all the ingredients

Stir gently to combine

Strain into a chilled glass

Garnish with a light dusting of grated nutmeg

CALVADOS COCKTAIL

I once drove an Aston Martin DB7 from my home in Sussex to Le Mans in France to watch the 24-hour race in the great company of Marek Reichman, the charismatic design director of Aston Martin. The engineering precision of Marek and his merry band of mechanical minds always amazes me; the speed their cars conjure is heady, the noise interstellar, but among my favourite moments of the trip was trundling through the orchards of Normandy stopping in the evenings to sip gently on cider and pick up cases of Calvados to bring home. This cocktail is a tribute to touring with good taste in great company.

45ml (1½oz) Calvados

15ml (½oz) triple sec

45ml (1½oz) orange juice

2 dashes orange bitters

Ice: Cubed

Garnish: Orange twist

Equipment: Cocktail shaker, strainer

Fill a shaker with ice

Add all the ingredients

Shake vigorously to chill

Strain into a chilled glass

Garnish with an orange twist

BRANDY MILK PUNCH

Vanilla and brandy are sublime. Oak is what gives brandy its colour and is often said to have a discreet whisper of vanilla along with other spices – it depends on how heavily toasted the barrel was, and the origin of the oak. Here, that mild, mellow infrastructure guides all the delights of dairy into a cooling, silky glass of sheer relaxation. It's often served in New Orleans with brunch, but is also ideal if you're in the mood for a nibble of chocolate – now that would be a delightful pairing. But this classic of the Prohibition era served on its own is one of life's greatest treats – and you deserve it.

45ml (1½oz) brandy

90ml (3oz) whole milk

7.5ml (¼oz) simple syrup (see page 11)

Dash/½ tsp of pure vanilla
    extract (optional)

Ice: Cubed

Garnish: Grated nutmeg

Equipment: Cocktail shaker, strainer

Fill a shaker with ice

Add all the ingredients

Shake vigorously to chill

Strain into a glass filled with ice

Garnish with a light dusting of grated nutmeg

This is also delicious if you swap the brandy for an aged rum. Up to seven years old is ample for the correct rich, smooth sweetness.

BRANDY COCKTAIL

This is one to whip up as though you are pushing a drinks trolley from the very best cocktail bar into your home. It has the hallmarks of greatness. An unbeatable cocktail to pour after a meal, it is as complex and reflective as the greatest novel as well as being as entertaining and stimulating as the finest conversation. Whether you are alone or in good company, settle in, sip steadily and reach ever deeper. This cocktail is the map that will guide your mind into the very depths of delight.

60ml (2oz) brandy

7.5ml (¼oz) Grand Marnier

7.5ml (¼oz) simple syrup (see page 11)

2 dashes Angostura Bitters

Ice: Cubed

Garnish: Orange twist

Equipment: Cocktail shaker, muddler and strainer

Fill a cocktail shaker with ice

Add all the ingredients and shake vigorously to chill

Strain into a chilled glass

Garnish with an orange twist

CHARLIE CHAPLIN

I have always been a Laurel and Hardy fan and as I get older, I embrace the genius of Charlie Chaplin more and more. I think the turning point was when I spotted a quote online that it was claimed came from the great man's notes: 'Imagination means nothing without doing.' This cocktail was created when he was at the peak of his powers in the early 20th century. You can add a little water to the shaker if you feel like a little more dilution, but cocktails are like comedy – we all have different tastes. Here's to having a laugh!

22.5ml (¾oz) apricot brandy

22.5ml (¾oz) sloe gin

22.5ml (¾oz) freshly squeezed lime juice

Ice: Cubed

Garnish: Apricot slice

Equipment: Cocktail shaker, strainer

Fill a shaker with ice

Add all the ingredients

Shake to chill and then shake some more – you need the ice to add a little dilution

Strain into a chilled glass

Garnish with an apricot slice

METROPOLITAN

If you're a fan of the Cosmopolitan, you'll love the Metropolitan. It may have an urban name and originate from New York in the 1990s, but I love drinking Metropolitans while sitting on hay bales at festivals, parties or picnics. It's an easy one to knock up and transport in a flask. Simply shake over ice and deliver all the sophistication of a lunchtime cocktail in a bustling metropolis and deploy it where you will. Riverside, atop a mountain, perhaps even gliding in a canoe. Just let the good times drift along with you.

60ml (2oz) brandy

30ml (1oz) sweet vermouth

7.5ml (¼oz) simple syrup (see page 11)

2 dashes Angostura Bitters

Ice: Cubed

Garnish: Orange twist

Equipment: Cocktail shaker, strainer

Fill a shaker with ice

Add all the ingredients

Shake vigorously to chill

Strain into a chilled glass

Garnish with an orange twist

DEAUVILLE #1

Normandy! Where the beaches are spread down the coast like golden butter, gentle hills roll into medieval spires and modest eateries become fables as days drift off into legends. The libation that links all of this magic is apple brandy, and at the heart of my Deauville I've united Calvados of the north with brandy of the south and all the charm of a French romance.

30ml (1oz) Calvados

30ml (1oz) brandy (ideally a Cognac)

30ml (1oz) triple sec

22.5ml (¾oz) freshly squeezed lemon juice

7.5ml (¼oz) simple syrup (see page 11)

Ice: Cubed

Garnish: Lemon twist

Equipment: Cocktail shaker, strainer

Fill a shaker with ice

Add all the ingredients

Shake vigorously to chill

Strain into a chilled glass

Garnish with a lemon twist

OLLY'S
APPLE COOLER

I have a young apple tree in my garden of a variety called Laxton's Fortune, around which I have planted a wildflower meadow on a hummock known to my friends and family as Laxton's Island. Laxton's Island overlooks two ancient apple trees that have become intertwined down the decades. One is a small tree with cooking apples, the other has large dessert apples; both were planted possibly half a century ago or more, and are now draped in lichen. They struggle to deliver fruit each year in the presence of male and female mistletoe, one in each tree.

Apples are an emblem of generosity linked with the industry of nature's gift: pollination. Bees roam my apple trees and while my two ancient friends may be fading, I take heart in the thought that Laxton's Island will be supplying pollen to visitors for many years to come. This drink is what I sip when I raise my glass to the familiar yet fabulous crunch of a freshly handpicked apple.

45ml (1½oz) Calvados

15ml (½oz) apple liqueur

7.5ml (¼oz) Goldschläger cinnamon schnapps

45ml (1½oz) cloudy apple juice

Soda water, to top

Ice: Cubed

Garnish: Apple slice

Equipment: Cocktail shaker, strainer

Fill a shaker with ice

Add all the ingredients except the soda water

Shake vigorously to chill

Strain into a glass filled with ice and top with soda water

Garnish with an apple slice

COGNAC CRUMBLE

Ginger and orange are echoed here by brandy and triple sec. Fluffed up with the egg white and garnished with a rim of crushed ginger snap biscuit, this cocktail is great fun. It's so easy to make at home and yet makes you look like a professional bartender. If you want to wow your friends and family with a guaranteed result, stick to the proportions of this recipe and your reward will be adulation.

60ml (2oz) brandy

15ml (½oz) triple sec

22.5ml (¾oz) orange juice

½ an egg white

Fiery ginger beer, to top

Ice: Cubed

Garnish: Crushed ginger snap biscuit rim and orange twist

Equipment: Cocktail shaker, strainer

Fill a shaker with ice

Add all the ingredients except the ginger beer

Shake vigorously to chill

Strain into glass filled with ice and top with ginger beer

Garnish with crushed ginger snap rim and a zested orange twist

COCTEL ALGERIA

I was once on a hair-raising adventure in North Africa which ranged between being chased by bandits to being asked by a conman to smuggle camera film in a bag of oranges. Much to his chagrin, I declined, and thus I devote this cocktail to memories of high jinks and hot days, when I learned one of life's simpler lessons: when somebody tells you they are a person of confidence, what they actually mean to say is: 'I am a confidence trickster.' This drink, however, is 100% reliable and always the best friend who welcomes you home after a bumpy ride.

45ml (1½oz) pisco

15ml (½oz) apricot liqueur

15ml (½oz) triple sec

30ml (1oz) orange juice

2 dashes orange bitters

Ice: Cubed

Garnish: Orange twist

Equipment: Cocktail shaker, strainer

Fill a shaker with ice

Add all the ingredients

Shake vigorously to chill

Strain into a chilled glass

Garnish with an orange twist

PISCO BELLRINGER

Ding dong! What a resonant, fruity cocktail this is. Exotic and aromatic Creole bitters, mellow, sweet apricot and scented, lively pisco combine in harmonious refreshment, summoning you to ascend the belltower of Cocktail Castle and hear the sound that says: 'Any time is Pisco Bellringer time.' Pull that rope!

60ml (2oz) pisco

15ml (½oz) freshly squeezed lemon juice

7.5ml (¼oz) simple syrup (see page 11)

Dash Creole bitters

Dash Angostura Bitters

7.5ml (¼oz) apricot liqueur

Ice: Cubed

Equipment: Cocktail shaker, strainer

Add all the ingredients except the apricot liqueur to a shaker filled with ice

Shake vigorously to chill

Rinse the inside of a chilled glass with the apricot liqueur and discard the excess

Strain the contents of the shaker into the glass

You can swap out the pisco for grappa.

A CALL TO ARMS

The first compact disc I ever bought was Dire Straits' *Brothers in Arms*. I remember being so impressed with the salesman in the video centre in St Helier, Jersey, when he dropped the CD on the carpeted floor, trod on it then placed it back into the stereo – and the music played perfectly. Up until that point cassettes and vinyl had been my world. Today cassettes and vinyl are still my world thanks to my devotion to retro sound systems, but I do still own the CD of *Brothers in Arms* and yes, it still plays. This cocktail is just as memorable, and once you've sipped it, it'll always be ready to rock in your library of libation.

45ml (1½oz) grappa

15ml (½oz) maraschino cherry liqueur

30ml (1oz) pink grapefruit juice

15ml (½oz) freshly squeezed lime juice

7.5ml (¼oz) red wine syrup (see page 11)

Soda water, to top

Ice: Cubed

Garnish: Grapefruit slice

Equipment: Cocktail shaker, strainer

Fill a shaker with ice

Add all the ingredients except the soda water

Shake vigorously to chill

Strain into a glass filled with ice

Slide the grapefruit slice garnish down the inside of the glass

Top with soda water

RUM

Rum! I am roaring to the Caribbean where this sweet spirit of sublime quality has been evolving for centuries. I always think of white sand beaches and easy warm days with rum in my glass, and there's something about the taste and its origins in sugar that give it instant deliciousness. It feels like a treat, yet how the sugar is treated has a big impact on the flavours in the rum.

One of the main bases for rum is molasses, a by-product of sugar production, which has a thick richness. The other is sugarcane juice, which produces rhum agricole, and which you could say is a little more connected with brandy in style, especially after it has been aged in old Cognac barrels. The Caribbean has many influences on other nations' rum traditions: for example, the British Navy used to dole it out as part of sailors' daily rations. Export and trade spreading across the world all bring further diversity to this libation's lexicon, and then there's production and ageing to consider and the impact they can have on cocktails.

If rum is produced in a pot still, it tends to be richer and suitable for ageing, resulting in contemplative complexity. Column stills tend to be for lighter rums, which are great for something a little more refreshing and fun. And young and old rums can be blended, which really means you need to be guided by taste – choose from easy and bright flavours right through to treacly and bold. If you're just

after one bottle to cover most bases for these cocktails, a three-year-old, good-quality rum – from the Caribbean, Latin America or even the UK – will be a perfect all-rounder for a marriage of sweet spirit with gently spiced wood. Texturally these rums have a light creaminess and a vanilla, smoky touch in the background. If a rum has been aged in the hot Caribbean, the rate of evaporation and intensification of the flavours happens more quickly than, say, a whisky would mature on a cold Scottish island, so the older rums really can deliver huge welly, which isn't always what you want when creating balanced cocktails. And the type of barrel used, such as an old bourbon cask, may have an influence. Stick to a three year old and your cocktails will all be classics.

I've also included cachaça in this section, which is a spirit associated with Brazil and close to a youthful rhum agricole. As for where the name rum comes from? Who knows for sure. There are some who say it's from 'rumbullion', an old word that loosely means a hullaballoo; others say it's from the Latin for sugar, 'saccharum', and it's also been suggested that Dutch 'roemer' drinking glasses dating from the 17th century may have been responsible. Perhaps the most colourful name for rum dates back to the 1620s – it was known as 'Kill-Devil' in the Caribbean. I can't guarantee any of these recipes will have that effect, but I'm confident they will all show you a devil of a good time!

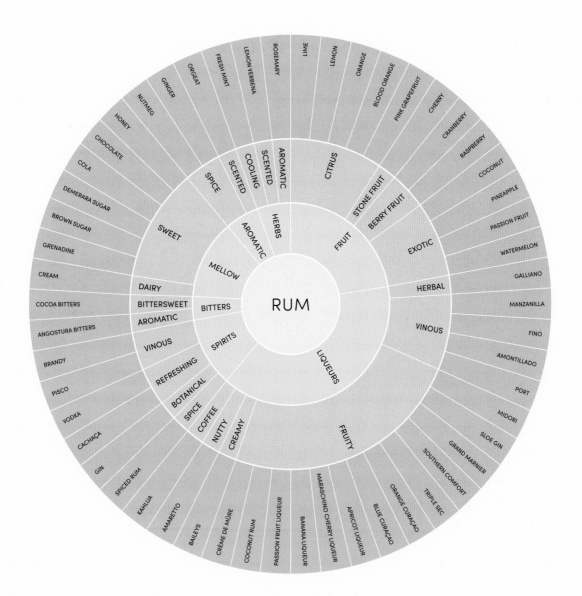

MARY PICKFORD

This was created for actress Mary Pickford back in the 1920s in Cuba. Mary's second of three marriages was to Douglas Fairbanks and they became known as the King and Queen of Hollywood, holding court from their Pickfair mansion in Beverly Hills. I've always loved drinks that are named after people – I guess Mary's status was the reason a drink was made in her honour. I can't see anyone drinking an Olly Smith any time soon, but perhaps they might drink a Bon Vivant. I love the light sweetness of rum – a three-year-old with that light infusion of spicy oak is a fantastic base for the long fruitiness of this drink. Everyone should have a signature drink – drink a Mary Pickford then try making one of your own!

45ml (1½oz) three-year-old rum

15ml (½oz) maraschino cherry liqueur

45ml (1½oz) pineapple juice

7.5ml (¼oz) grenadine

Ice: Cubed

Garnish: Maraschino cherry

Equipment: Cocktail shaker, strainer

Fill a shaker with ice

Add all the ingredients

Shake vigorously to chill

Strain into a chilled glass

Garnish with a speared maraschino cherry

DAIQUIRI (UP)

The basic elements of a Daiquiri are rum, citrus and sweet.

Once you've mastered the recipe try different syrups or juices to create your own. This classic take on the Daiquiri hones the sweet, sharp, spirit trinity to perfection and 'up' – shaken with ice and served in a chilled glass – is the way to behold the true heavenly calibre of this mixture. Whenever I make one of these, I can guarantee that my wife Sophie will take a sip, and before she's blinked will be asking for a Daiquiri of her own. It's a staple at Smith Towers.

60ml (2oz) seven-year-old rum

30ml (1oz) freshly squeezed lime juice

15ml (½oz) simple syrup made with demerara sugar (see page 11)

Ice: Cubed

Garnish: Lime twist

Equipment: Cocktail shaker, strainer

Fill a shaker with ice

Add all the ingredients

Shake vigorously until the shaker is frosted

Strain into a chilled glass

Garnish with a lime twist

HEMINGWAY

If you're being a purist then you should omit the simple syrup from this recipe, since Ernest Hemingway himself was diabetic. But in my view it leaves the drink searingly dry, which presumably Hemingway found thirst-quenchingly delightful.

I've always loved the overlays of sharp, sweet and spirit that Daiquiris deliver. For some reason their harmonious intrigue always makes me feel like I'm in a bar on a great adventure in a far-flung corner of the world. Sometimes I have been known to wear a safari jacket when sipping on a Daiquiri: my dad's ancient one from the 1970s which he bought in M&S, to be precise. I'm not sure it adds much to the experience except being a distant reminder that somewhere, the weather is always warmer. There is simply no other cocktail like a Daiquiri and while it has been cast as a sweet, lurid, fruity concoction, making one at home in this form shows its true class and poise. You can't help but feel inspired to share tales after one, and in my view, this recipe is the ultimate Daiquiri of delight. Hemingway was someone who lived life to the full and was a person of extremes. This drink happily avoids the pitfalls while delivering all the passion.

60ml (2oz) three-year-old rum

15ml (½oz) maraschino cherry liqueur

22.5ml (¾oz) freshly squeezed lime juice

15ml (½oz) grapefruit juice

7.5ml (¼oz) simple syrup (see page 11)

Ice: Cubed

Garnish: Lime wedge

Equipment: Cocktail shaker, strainer

Fill a shaker with ice

Add all the ingredients

Shake vigorously to chill

Strain into a chilled glass

Garnish with a lime wedge

This is the most famous of all Daiquiri recipes – think King Kong in a world of great apes.

OLLY DAIQUIRI

Ernest Hemingway famously came up with his own signature Daiquiri using maraschino cherry and grapefruit as the key ingredients. Taste my signature Olly Daiquiri for a simple, scrumptious alternative. Using a bunch of my personal favourite flavours, it's easy and precise, and if I do say myself, it's tastier than Hemingway's. Whether it'll end up sipped as widely worldwide, time will tell. It's great to make at home, and I also recommend photographing the recipe for an Olly Daiquiri to take to parties and bars to make sure you can always get a ready supply. It really is utterly splendid!

60ml (2oz) Havana Club Especial rum (double aged)

22.5ml (¾oz) freshly squeezed blood orange juice

22.5ml (¾oz) freshly squeezed pink grapefruit juice

7.5ml (¼oz) red wine syrup (see page 11)

1 tsp soft brown sugar (or simple syrup made with demerara sugar; see page 11)

Ice: Cubed

Garnish: Orange twist

Equipment: Cocktail shaker, strainer

Fill a shaker with ice

Add all the ingredients

Shake vigorously until the shaker is frosted

Strain into a chilled glass

Garnish with an orange twist

DARK & STORMY™

My friend Tom Cara has the world's largest ginger beard and loves this cocktail even more than he loves his hairiness. He's a proud citizen of Glasgow, and most Fridays I'll receive a text from him which involves his latest twist on this spicy sipper. It's amazingly easy to make: ginger and rum are a hand-in-glove pairing thanks to their common spectrum of sweet spiciness, and are as close as apples and pears. They adore one another. Imagine a magnet with both ends attracting – that's what rum and ginger beer do to each other. They form a ring of perfect resonance.

60ml (2oz) dark rum

15ml (½oz) freshly squeezed lime juice

7.5ml (¼oz) simple syrup (see page 11)

120ml (4oz) fiery ginger beer, to top

Ice: Crushed

Garnish: Lime wedge

Equipment: Long bar spoon

Fill a glass two-thirds with crushed ice

Add all the ingredients except the ginger beer

Stir gently to combine

Top with the ginger beer and cap with more crushed ice

Garnish with a lime wedge

To make a **Stormy Seas**, replace the dark rum with spiced rum.

PLANTER'S PUNCH

A classic rum cocktail! Planter's Punch to rum is what Sherlock Holmes is to crime busting. Legend has it this drink first appeared in the *New York Times* in 1908 – all I can say for sure is that this version appeared in 2021 in my garden while an inquisitive robin perched on my side table peering longingly at my nibbles. I always think of this as a jolly cocktail, a cheery beverage, the kind of thing you should drink to celebrate good fortune. And since you're going to the trouble of making it, it's only fitting that you should relax and survey your liquid empire of excellence before you raise a glass silently to your excellent endeavour. Here's to you!

45ml (1½oz) dark rum

22.5ml (¾oz) pineapple juice

22.5ml (¾oz) orange juice

7.5ml (¼oz) grenadine

Soda water, to top (optional)

Ice: Cubed

Garnish: Pineapple wedge

Equipment: Cocktail shaker, strainer

Fill a shaker with ice

Add all the ingredients except the soda water

Shake vigorously to chill

Strain into a glass filled with ice and top with soda water, if you want a little sparkle

Garnish with a pineapple wedge

PAINKILLER™

An absolute classic, and often sipped as a cure for the condition my dear granny used to describe as being 'rough in the cheek' (also known as the morning after the night before). For a cocktail to qualify as a Painkiller, Pusser's Rum must be used – it's even been trademarked. Now, much as I recommend avoiding them altogether, hangovers may occasionally occur. With this drink, rather than thinking of it as a restorative, I love to sip it late in the afternoon to inspire me to greater depth in the moment. One or two of these is a top way to drift gently from working hard to surfing your mind into the calm of an easy evening ahead.

45ml (1½oz) Pusser's Rum

90ml (3oz) pineapple juice

22.5ml (¾oz) orange juice

22.5ml (¾oz) coconut cream

Ice: Cubed

Garnish: Pineapple wedge and grated nutmeg

Equipment: Cocktail shaker, strainer

Fill a shaker with ice

Add all the ingredients

Shake vigorously to chill

Strain into a glass filled with ice

Garnish with a pineapple wedge and dust with grated nutmeg

RUMBUNCTIOUS

With a Rumbunctious in your grasp, you can navigate the high seas of deliciousness. The cocoa bitters take this off the charts and the spice in the rum elevates it to a riot of refreshment that's enhanced with the fire of ginger beer. Pineapple juice and lime set the tiller on course for the Islands of Ease, and you'll find one of these settles very nicely into two. All aboard for the long haul!

45ml (1½oz) spiced rum

15ml (½oz) pineapple juice

1 lime, cut into 6 pieces

2 dashes cocoa bitters

60ml (2oz) fiery ginger beer, to top

Ice: Cubed

Garnish: Lime wheel

Equipment: Cocktail shaker, muddler and strainer

Muddle the lime in the bottom of a shaker

Add ice along with the remaining ingredients except the ginger beer

Shake to chill

Strain into a glass filled with ice and top with the ginger beer

Garnish with a lime wheel

BEACHCOMBER

You could think of this as a delicious diversion from a Daiquiri. The Beachcomber embraces the magic of maraschino cherry liqueur and feels like a classy alternative. I've always felt it marries the spirit of the beach with the elegance of fine dining and I love drinking one al fresco – I've even put together a Beachcomber on the pebbles of Seaford Beach in Sussex, although any open window with a half-decent view will do. Whatever the weather, the Beachcomber will always make you feel warm inside.

60ml (2oz) three-year-old rum

22.5ml (¾oz) triple sec

7.5ml (¼oz) maraschino cherry liqueur

22.5ml (¾oz) freshly squeezed lime juice

Dash simple syrup (see page 11), optional

Ice: Cubed

Garnish: Lime wedge

Equipment: Cocktail shaker, strainer

Fill a shaker with ice

Add all the ingredients

Shake vigorously to chill

Strain into a chilled glass

Garnish with a lime wedge

Add a dash of simple syrup if you find the drink is not sweet enough.

PS I LOVE YOU

This amalgamates all the great things in life: rum, which makes me think of being on holiday with my wife in St Lucia with cold cocktails framing the days; Baileys, which my wife likes to go swimming in; Kahlua, which I adore as an after-dinner digestif; and amaretto, which everyone secretly worships. And cream. Great fun! Chocolate powder gives it the allure of a pudding with delectable silky sumptuousness. For a spot of indulgence, PS I Love You is perfect instead of a dessert at a dinner party or for a special-occasion treat. I think the best way to enjoy it is with a cream tea. Outrageous!

15ml (½oz) three-year-old rum

15ml (½oz) Baileys

15ml (½oz) Kahlua

15ml (½oz) amaretto

15ml (½oz) single (light) cream

Ice: Cubed

Garnish: Chocolate powder

Equipment: Cocktail shaker, strainer

Fill a shaker with ice

Add all the ingredients

Shake vigorously to chill

Strain into a chilled glass

Garnish with a sprinkle of chocolate powder

CITRUS RUM COOLER

A cooler should be as brilliant and exhilarating as skydiving through a giant lightbulb. Brighten your day with this gorgeous zinger. The inspiration for this drink was a similar rum-based cooler I found myself sipping in a Melbourne bar while working with the England cricket team on the 2013/14 Ashes tour of Australia. My drink kept me refreshed in the heat and inspired great fun even in Ashes defeat – especially as my job included taking part in a fishing competition with Sir Ian 'Beefy' Botham. Both he and Australia may have won by a small margin, but the cocktails that flowed were every bit as tasty as the cold local Chardonnay that kept us quenched as we left port. And returning to land made my own personal defeat on the high seas all the more palatable.

37.5ml (1¼oz) three-year-old rum

15ml (½oz) Grand Marnier

60ml (2oz) freshly squeezed orange juice

7.5ml (¼oz) freshly squeezed lime juice

Lemonade, to top

Ice: Cubed

Garnish: Lemon wedge and lime wedge

Equipment: Cocktail shaker, strainer

Fill a shaker with ice

Add all ingredients except the lemonade

Shake vigorously to chill

Strain into a glass filled with ice and top with lemonade

Garnish with a lemon wedge and lime wedge

WATERMELON COOLER

While this drink itself doesn't contain actual watermelon, it's nice to serve a slice on the side to eat – I reckon it's one of the most cooling fruits out there. Midori in this recipe is where the might of watermelon asserts itself; the word 'Midori' in Japanese means 'green', which reflects the almost luminous colour of this lush liqueur. The key flavour it brings is luscious, sweet melon – there's nothing diluted about it. The sour slice of citrus and cranberry balance it out in this recipe and work a charm. And it always amazes me how a little Midori goes a long way in a cocktail – it's just oozing presence. Now, when I tell you that Midori was launched in the USA at a party for the cast and crew of *Saturday Night Fever*, when according to legend it was mixed with tonic, you know that with with one of these in your hand you should be dancing!

37.5ml (1¼oz) three-year-old rum

22.5ml (¾oz) Midori

75ml (2½oz) cranberry juice

30ml (1oz) orange juice

7.5ml (¼oz) freshly squeezed lime juice

Ice: Cubed

Garnish: Mint sprig

Equipment: Cocktail shaker, strainer

Fill a shaker with ice

Add all the ingredients

Shake vigorously to chill

Strain into a glass filled with ice

Garnish with a sprig of mint

HONEY BEE

I kept honeybees for years, and I'm a patron of the Bumblebee Conservation Trust. I love honey as much as I love bees. One of the more common misconceptions is that we need more bees, particularly in cities. Actually, there's often not enough forage to feed our existing bees, which come in all shapes and sizes from solitary to bumblebees. Dumping more and more bees in one place creates too much competition for scarce food supplies. What we need is to create space for more pollinator-friendly plants, whether on rooftops or road verges, in window boxes or back gardens. Honey that's high in pollen is always my favourite as it's so full of flavour, and you could pick one that's been influenced by a certain plant, whether that's acacia, heather or manuka. Honey is like wine in that it will always reflect its place. Bees are incredible – vital, in fact, to various sensitive ecosystems around the world and for production of our fruit and veg. They work for free and they enrich our lives in a world of pressured natural habitat. So all I ask when you make this cocktail at home is that you raise your glass and promise to be a bit more bee. Go wild.

60ml (2oz) dark rum

22.5ml (¾oz) honey simple syrup (see page 11)

15ml (½oz) freshly squeezed lemon juice

7.5ml (¼oz) orange juice (optional)

Ice: Cubed

Garnish: Lemon twist

Equipment: Cocktail shaker, strainer

Fill a shaker with ice

Add all the ingredients

Shake vigorously to chill

Strain into a chilled glass

Garnish with a lemon twist

Add the orange juice to taste if you wish.

PARASOL

I spent some time teaching English in Sumatra, Indonesia, at the University of Jambi. While the sun was pretty hot in the tropics, I never deployed a physical parasol. I used to drink a version of this drink instead to keep cool. Thankfully pineapple was in great supply, and I made my own banana liqueur with a bit of patience and ingenuity by soaking bananas in rum for a few days. I'm not sure how good my English teaching was after drinking a homemade Parasol or two, but this recipe is even better and will keep you fluent in your native tongue (and almost certainly the international language of dance as well). Get grooving!

60ml (2oz) three-year-old rum

22.5ml (¾oz) banana liqueur

22.5ml (¾oz) freshly squeezed lime juice

15ml (½oz) pineapple juice

Ice: Cubed

Garnish: Pineapple wedge

Equipment: Cocktail shaker, strainer

Fill a shaker with ice

Add all the ingredients

Shake vigorously until the shaker is frosted

Strain into a chilled glass

Garnish with a pineapple wedge

SCORPION

I've had two close shaves with scorpions. The first time was when I was a kid growing up in Jersey in the Channel Islands. On the tarmac of Clos des Blanches estate something small, shiny and black with claws and a rearing, piercing tail was scuttling and posing. It ran away before my friends and I had time to alert any parents. Looking back, it must have been a scorpion imposter as I'm pretty sure they aren't found in the Channel Islands – either way, it stuck in my mind. The second was in Greece, an orange little thing, waiting for me when I got home from a taverna in the porch of my rented accommodation. I was as terrified as I was enthralled as it scurried into the darkness. You don't need to be terrified of this drink, just feel its thrill. It is really easy to make, and that judicious addition of orgeat makes it even more delicious than you can imagine – and there's no sting in the tail.

45ml (1½oz) three-year-old rum

22.5ml (¾oz) brandy

45ml (1½oz) freshly squeezed orange juice

15ml (½oz) freshly squeezed lemon juice

7.5ml (¼oz) orgeat

Ice: Crushed

Garnish: Orange slice and mint sprig

Equipment: Blender

Add a scoop of crushed ice to a blender cup

Add all the ingredients

Blend until smooth

Tap into a glass

Garnish with an orange slice and sprig of mint

You can use pisco instead of rum.

JUNE BUG

Who doesn't love a bright green cocktail? Like the Blue Hawaii this is an ideal party drink. If you like things on the sweeter side, this is the perfect drink for you. It's a great cocktail to unleash at parties, partly because it's fun and scrumptious, mainly because green drinks are the best drinks! It's named after a type of beetle that appears in June – there are, in fact, lots of different types of (insect) June bugs. One thing they all have in common is that they like hanging around electric lights in porches, so if you're drawn to the brighter things in life like those little bugs, drink this and feel illumination from the inside out. And unlike those beetles, this particular June Bug loves to come out all year round!

22.5ml (¾oz) coconut rum

22.5ml (¾oz) Midori

22.5ml (¾oz) banana liqueur

90ml (3oz) pineapple juice

15ml (½oz) freshly squeezed lime juice

Ice: Cubed

Garnish: Pineapple wedge

Equipment: Cocktail shaker, strainer

Fill a shaker with ice

Add all the ingredients

Shake vigorously to chill

Strain into a glass filled with ice

Garnish with a pineapple wedge

RUM

PINO PEPE

This is one of those cocktails that is deceptively drinkable but packs quite a punch. It was after drinking one of these I decided to learn how to juggle and found I already could. Limes, it turns out, seem to be magnets to my palms. I'm always drawn to citrus flavours with rum, I guess from my inherent adoration of the Daiquiri. The sharp, cutting spell of anything with brisk acidity is such a complement to rum's mellow sugarcane roots. With the bright swipe of pineapple and vodka, my Pino Pepe is a proper sabre of sunlight to cut into your kitchen and set the night ablaze.

30ml (1oz) three-year-old rum

30ml (1oz) vodka

15ml (½oz) triple sec

30ml (1oz) pineapple juice

15ml (½oz) freshly squeezed lime juice

7.5ml (¼oz) freshly squeezed lemon juice

7.5ml (¼oz) simple syrup (see page 11)

Ice: Crushed

Garnish: Lime wedge

Equipment: Blender

Add a scoop of crushed ice to a blender cup

Add all the ingredients

Blend until smooth

Tap into a wine glass or tiki glass, if you have one

Garnish with a lime wedge

ZOMBIE

In my experience, the Zombie has the opposite effect to what its name might suggest – in fact, rather than zombify, it'll more likely turn you into the most erudite person at the party, capable of balletic dance moves worthy of Darcey Bussell herself. Sure, this is a boozy cocktail, and contains four lively liquors in a full-throttle, tiki-type incarnation. It's said to have its origins in 1930s Hollywood – and I've always felt the Zombie is a vintage icon worthy of greater plaudits. Think of all the star zombies in movies – *Night of the Living Dead*, *Dawn of the Dead*, *28 Days Later* – they all stand on their own. For some reason, the Zombie as a drink is either thought of as being a bit silly or too strong to be able to deploy. But there's no better time than now to embrace the gravitas of an iconic cocktail that'll live forever.

22.5ml (¾oz) dark rum

22.5ml (¾oz) three-year-old rum

15ml (½oz) apricot liqueur

15ml (½oz) orange curaçao

60ml (2oz) pineapple juice

7.5ml (¼oz) freshly squeezed lemon juice

Dash orgeat

Ice: Cubed

Garnish: Pineapple wedge

Equipment: Cocktail shaker, strainer

Fill a shaker with ice

Add all the ingredients

Shake vigorously to chill

Strain into a glass filled with ice

Garnish with a pineapple wedge

For an extra kick float 15ml (½oz) of overproof 151 rum (flaming if you dare!).

HURRICANE

I was once caught in very high seas in a ship in the Caribbean Sea, rattling around like a frozen pea in an empty baked bean tin. I remember consoling myself and banishing any thought that the ship might go down by thinking of calmer waters and the chance to raise a Hurricane to my brush with Neptune's rage. Who knows whether this cocktail is named after the storm, the shape of the glass or a particular bar? All I know is that my version has the power of a force 10 gale with none of the rolling of the horizon from one side to the other. In fact, the only shaking you'll need to do is with the shaker and it's so worth it to blend the two rums in this cocktail. The seven-year-old brings wood spice and richness, the three-year-old a lighter fruitiness – almost like blending a sultana with a grape. Once that storm had passed, I remember my friend Nestor and I raising Hurricanes to the hurricane we'd managed to come through. It's a drink of gratitude, a reminder that things can change fast, and in the case of this drink it's always a change for the better.

30ml (1oz) three-year-old rum

30ml (1oz) seven-year-old rum

45ml (1½oz) pineapple juice

30ml (1oz) orange juice

15ml (½oz) freshly squeezed lime juice

15ml (½oz) passion fruit juice or purée

7.5ml (¼oz) simple syrup (see page 11)

Ice: Cubed

Garnish: Pineapple wedge and orange slice

Equipment: Cocktail shaker, strainer

Fill a shaker with ice

Add all the ingredients

Shake vigorously to chill

Strain into a glass filled with ice

Garnish with a pineapple wedge and slice of orange

BETWEEN
THE SHEETS

A real Prohibition-era classic, this will appeal to lovers of cocktails such as the Sidecar and Maiden's Prayer, which follow similar lines to this recipe (or diverge with gin versions). This historic sequencing of spirits, citrus, sweetness and liqueur will invoke the rowdy, carefree mood of a speakeasy. Equal measures of the boozy ingredients set up a frame for even parts citrus to syrup – invoking harmony and, as the name suggests, good times ahead.

22.5ml (¾oz) three-year-old rum

22.5ml (¾oz) brandy

22.5ml (¾oz) triple sec

7.5ml (¼oz) freshly squeezed lemon juice

7.5ml (¼oz) simple syrup (see page 11)

Ice: Cubed

Garnish: Lemon twist

Equipment: Cocktail shaker, strainer

Fill a shaker with ice

Add all the ingredients

Shake vigorously to chill

Strain into a chilled glass

Garnish with a lemon twist

FROZEN FRUIT DAIQUIRI

When was the last time you watched *Top Gun*? Probably around the same time you last had a Frozen Fruit Daiquiri! Both are evergreen classics, both are completely entertaining and brilliant, and both make you feel cooler than you probably are. Stick *Top Gun* on the screen and a Frozen Fruit Daiquiri in your glass and you'll be playing with the boys before you know it.

45ml (1½oz) three-year-old rum

15ml (½oz) fruit liqueur (that matches the fruit purée of your choice)

30ml (1oz) fruit purée of your choice

15ml (½oz) freshly squeezed lime juice

7.5ml (¼oz) simple syrup (see page 11)

Ice: Crushed

Garnish: Speared frozen fruits of your choice

Equipment: Blender

Add a scoop of crushed ice to a blender cup

Add all the ingredients

Blend until smooth

Tap the blender as you pour to coax the drink into the glass

Garnish with the fruit of your choice

Frozen daiquiris are a great way to experiment with fruit flavours.

BLUE HAWAII

Not to be confused with the Blue Hawaiian that follows, this exotic dream of a drink is as memorable as singing duets with Elvis in his prime. That gentle bed of voices supporting the rippling croon of the King in the song 'Blue Hawaii' reminds me of the layered loveliness of this delicious drink. When holidays seem far away, this cocktail is the liquid alternative. A trip to the tropics is only a few short shakes away. With its simple garnish, it's also a spectacle that implies so much more effort has gone into it than actually has, so pull up a front row seat for the show!

30ml (1oz) three-year-old rum

22.5ml (¾oz) vodka

15ml (½oz) blue curaçao

90ml (3oz) pineapple juice

15ml (½oz) freshly squeezed lime juice

15ml (½oz) freshly squeezed lemon juice

7.5ml (¼oz) simple syrup (see page 11)

Ice: Cubed

Garnish: Pineapple-cherry sail

Equipment: Cocktail shaker, strainer

Fill a shaker with ice

Add all the ingredients

Shake vigorously to chill

Strain into a glass filled with ice

Garnish with a pineapple-cherry sail

BLUE HAWAIIAN

Not to be confused with the Blue Hawaii, this creamy classic is the stuff of legends. It's so much fun – a blue drink always leads to a brilliant time, because it's impossible for the moment not to rise into a soulful silliness which, in this case, leads to a taste of real refinement. As soon as coconut appears in a cocktail recipe, for some reason it's treated like a bit of a joke. I love it, though. In fact, it's the perfect punchline for when you've had enough of sophisticated Martinis and Sidecars. The aquamarine colour makes me think of surfing, a sport of poise and focus, much like the surprising splendour of the Blue Hawaiian itself. Catch the wave!

30ml (1oz) three-year-old rum

30ml (1oz) blue curaçao

90ml (3oz) pineapple juice

30ml (1oz) cream of coconut

7.5ml (¼oz) freshly squeezed lime juice

Ice: Crushed

Garnish: Pineapple-cherry sail

Equipment: Blender

Add a scoop of crushed ice to a blender cup

Add all the ingredients

Blend until smooth

Tap into a glass

Garnish with a pineapple-cherry sail (and a paper umbrella if you really want to go to town!)

SARAH'S CHRISTMAS PARTY

Sarah's Christmas party is the stuff of legends. You can picture the scene: feather boas, Frankie Goes to Hollywood blaring on the stereo, Twiglets everywhere, tinsel draped on all the guests, and Sarah herself at the heart of the madness, always with a glass of this favourite cocktail in her hand. I won't reveal her true identity to save her blushes; suffice to say that her original version of the cocktail is what I would describe as 'liquid jazz' – she made it up as she went along. Here, I have established rules for it, so when you throw your own Christmas party, this is the perfect festive frolic to serve to your guests. But why wait till Christmas? With this drink, it can be Christmas every day. Just ask Sarah.

45ml (1½oz) pineapple rum

15ml (½oz) Goldschläger cinnamon schnapps

30ml (1oz) orange juice

30ml (1oz) pineapple juice

7.5ml (¼oz) cinnamon simple syrup (see page 11)

Dash Angostura Bitters

Ice: Cubed

Garnish: Pineapple slice, orange slice and cherry

Equipment: Cocktail shaker, strainer

Fill a shaker with ice

Add all the ingredients

Shake vigorously to chill

Strain into a glass filled with ice

Garnish with a slice of pineapple, a slice of orange and a cherry

If you don't have pineapple rum to hand, it's fine to substitute with plain rum.

CUBA LIBRE

So much more than just a rum and Coke, thanks to the dash of Angostura and the easiness the drink conveys. The method here is key – you'll find the generous amount of lime as well as the gentle effort of muddling is transformative. Cuba's heritage is immense, from the music and automobiles to the cigars, buildings, politics and, of course, Pierce Brosnan pouting through the sunsets in the Bond film *GoldenEye*. There's a corner of Cuba for everyone – and this is your passport to those steamy vibes to chill with at home.

60ml (2oz) three-year-old rum

½ a lime, cut into 4 wedges

Dash Angostura Bitters

120ml (4oz) cola, to top

Ice: Cubed

Equipment: Long bar spoon

Muddle the lime wedges in a glass

Fill the glass with ice

Add the rum and bitters

Stir gently to combine

Top with the cola

To make a **Santo Libre**, replace the cola with a lemon-lime soda.

RUM PASSION

Passion fruit is among the most exotic flavours of all time. I remember the first time I saw passion fruit I thought it was alien eggs – thank goodness the taste is so sublimely scintillating. The zing of passion fruit juice brings this fantastic drink to life. The rich sweetness of coconut rum and passion fruit liqueur bind and thrive in tropical titillation. And while it may have the impact and curiosity of seeing a UFO, this drink is as far from alienation as can be. Make friends with it!

45ml (1½oz) coconut rum

15ml (½oz) passion fruit liqueur

30ml (1oz) passion fruit juice

15ml (½oz) freshly squeezed lime juice

Soda water, to top

Ice: Cubed

Garnish: Passion fruit half

Equipment: Cocktail shaker, strainer

Fill a shaker with ice

Add all the ingredients except the soda water

Shake vigorously to chill

Strain into a glass filled with ice and top with soda water

Garnish with half a passion fruit

LEMON VERBENA MOJITO

A refreshingly light and subtly flavoured alternative to the traditional Mojito.

Lemon verbena is one of my all-time favourite herbs to use in any cocktail because of its high-citrus exotic scent. It grows with great enthusiasm in my garden and manages to pull through most winters to supply its unique taste in summer. When I can, I like to make this recipe using fresh lemon verbena, and of course you can also buy them to use at home. Watch out when you muddle them: lemon verbena releases the most wonderful aroma and has been known to lure and entice party guests to my garden from beyond a two-mile radius. They seem to follow the scent like duty-free holidaymakers to the perfume counter. And the reward is incredible when you sip it. Such a simple change and yet the whole cocktail is transformed. Change it up!

45ml (1½oz) three-year-old rum

22.5ml (¾oz) freshly squeezed lime juice

15ml (½oz) lemon verbena syrup (see herb syrups, page 11)

6–8 lemon verbena leaves

Soda water, to top

Ice: Cubed

Garnish: Lemon verbena sprig

Equipment: Muddler, long bar spoon

Muddle the lemon verbena leaves in a glass

Fill the glass with ice

Add all the ingredients except the soda water

Churn gently to chill and mix

Top with soda water

Garnish with a lemon verbena sprig

MOJITO

Enduring and beloved and perhaps even more popular than the Moon landings, summer holidays and Aretha Franklin's greatest hits combined. There are claims that the Mojito stretches back centuries. While it certainly wasn't sipped by the ancient Aztecs, it was the year 2000 when the Mojito really soared in popularity, like a helicopter made of golden goodness. And as far as skills go, it relies on churning – keep your movement steady and gentle. If you do it too fast the ice will dilute, too slowly and the flavours won't blend seamlessly. The key to a top Mojito is balance – which is what makes it so beguilingly easy to sip, especially as a cold cocktail before a summer barbecue. Mint and rum never duel, they love one another in a dalliance of equal intensity – and combined with bubbly soda, the mighty Mojito is as effervescent as it is crowd-pleasing. Commence churning!

45ml (1½oz) three-year-old rum

22.5ml (¾oz) freshly squeezed lime juice

15ml (½oz) simple syrup (see page 11)

6–8 mint leaves

Soda water, to top

Ice: Crushed

Garnish: Mint sprig

Equipment: Muddler, long bar spoon

Muddle the mint leaves in a glass

Fill the glass two-thirds with crushed ice

Add all the ingredients except the soda water

Churn gently to chill

Top with soda water and cap with crushed ice

Garnish with a mint sprig

CAIPIRINHA

The first time I had cachaça I felt like a billy goat at the peak of a mountain wearing a jetpack. I leaped and orbited my own mind three times before landing back and realising what a splendid spirit it is. Underrated and awesome, cachaça has the immediacy of a fanfare with all of the enduring appeal of lounging lakeside on a day off. It is lift-off in a glass thanks to the spirited raw power it draws from freshly pressed sugarcane juice (rum is more often made from molasses). Relaxing with one of these has got to be one of the greatest pleasures in life. I love drinking them most of all with my friend Chloë, who paints in a crab shed on the North Norfolk coast. Come rain or shine, drinking Caipirinhas in Chloë's studio makes Wells-next-the-Sea feel like Rio de Janeiro, and be warned, a few of these can turn your living room into a carnival.

60ml (2oz) cachaça

¾ of a lime, cut into 6 pieces

2 bar spoons soft brown sugar

Ice: Crushed

Garnish: Lime wedge

Equipment: Muddler, long bar spoon

Muddle the limes and brown sugar in a glass

Fill the glass three-quarters with crushed ice and pour over the cachaça

Churn gently to chill and cap with more crushed ice

Garnish with a lime wedge

To make a **Caipiroska** simply exchange the cachaça for vodka and the brown sugar for white.

MAI TAI

Who can forget History's hip-swinging 80s classic hit 'Mai Tai'? The punchy synthesized beat and bold keyboard are spot-on for a gentle start to a kitchen disco, cocktail in hand. And that cocktail must be a Mai Tai! The secret to the mighty Mai Tai is that the key ingredient is always orange curaçao, which is based on the laraha citrus fruit (think orange to the power of ten). The effect adds fulsome flavour to a cocktail that's as rich as it is refreshing. This 20th-century drink is shrouded in mystery; it was made famous by the Trader Vic's chain of restaurants, which was founded by one Victor Jules Bergeron who opened the first in 1934. According to legend, Victor created this in 1944 and while the origin has been disputed, Trader Vic certainly made the Mai Tai his own. I've added my twist here by including pineapple juice. Make it, crank up the stereo and raise your glass to sunny splendour.

45ml (1½oz) three-year-old rum

22.5ml (¾oz) orange curaçao

60ml (2oz) pineapple juice

15ml (½oz) freshly squeezed lime juice

7.5ml (¼oz) orgeat

Dash grenadine

Ice: Cubed

Garnish: Lime wheel, mint sprig and pineapple wedge

Equipment: Cocktail shaker, strainer

Fill a shaker with ice

Add all the ingredients

Shake vigorously to chill

Strain into a glass filled with ice

Garnish with a lime wheel, mint sprig and pineapple wedge

RUM RUNNER

What is a Rum Runner, you may ask? It certainly isn't the 100-metre sprint after a tot or two of liquor. Rum running is the illegal business of smuggling booze to avoid taxation. Such naughtiness is, of course, frowned on in this saintly bible: only strictly lawful behaviour is encouraged between these pages. Now, you may have read the ingredients for the Rum Runner and thought, is it really worth combining all these? Absolutely it is – just think of it like the movie *Avengers Assemble*. Thanks to the perfect balance of superstars in this recipe, the only effort you need to put in is to pay close attention to your measurements. It's the precision in my Rum Runner that makes it so absolutely fantastic, and while I'm always encouraging you to experiment with your own cocktails, in this case I've done all the running for you.

15ml (½oz) crème de mûre

15ml (½oz) banana liqueur

15ml (½oz) freshly squeezed lime juice

7.5ml (¼oz) freshly squeezed lemon juice

7.5ml (¼oz) simple syrup (see page 11)

Dash grenadine

45ml (1½oz) three-year-old rum

Ice: Crushed

Garnish: Float of dark rum

Equipment: Blender

Add a scoop of crushed ice to a blender cup

Add all the ingredients except the three-year-old rum

Blend until smooth

Tip from the blender cup into the glass (you may need to tap the blender cup a few times) then float the rum on top

---

This can be shaken and poured over ice if you don't want a blended drink.

FOG CUTTER

No two ways about it, this is a pokey blend that will sharpen your mind into great concentration, away from the fog of the daily grind. With the addition of sherry, I've made this drink my own through my love of that underrated fortified wine from southern Spain. I'm using amontillado, which has a certain nutty richness, but feel free to experiment with bright, refreshing fino, or you could use the even lighter manzanilla if you prefer. Sherry's balance of savoury umami with natural zip is a proper palate reviver and I always love pouring Fog Cutters after long wine-tasting sessions. It's the perfect drink to jumpstart your taste buds.

37.5ml (1¼oz) three-year-old rum

15ml (½oz) gin

15ml (½oz) brandy

60ml (2oz) freshly squeezed orange juice

15ml (½oz) freshly squeezed lemon juice

Dash orgeat

15ml (½oz) amontillado sherry

Ice: Cubed

Garnish: Mint sprig and lemon twist

Equipment: Cocktail shaker, strainer

Fill a shaker with ice

Add all the ingredients except the sherry

Shake vigorously to chill

Strain into a glass filled with ice and float the sherry on top

Garnish with a sprig of mint and a lemon twist

Try substituting the sherry for red wine syrup (see page 11) to change it up.

WHITE LION

The White Lion is a historic drink with its roots in the late 1800s. Iconic as the three-piece suit, which came into fashion around the same time along with simple A-line skirts, this classy cocktail is guaranteed to appeal to lovers of the Daiquiri. Its flavours are turned all the way up to 11. Grenadine helps round out the generous flavours in this recipe and supports the resonance of the raspberry syrup by wrapping a bow around the sweet rum and citrus splendour. Making it and sipping it feels smart: skirts and suits are optional.

45ml (1½oz) seven-year-old rum

15ml (½oz) triple sec

7.5ml (¼oz) raspberry syrup

¾ of a lime, cut into 6 pieces

Dash grenadine

Ice: Cubed

Garnish: Frozen seasonal berries

Equipment: Cocktail shaker, muddler and strainer

Muddle the lime in the bottom of a shaker

Top with ice

Add the remaining ingredients

Shake vigorously until the shaker is frosted

Strain into a glass filled with ice

Garnish with frozen berries

YELLOWBIRD

The Yellowbird has enjoyed great popularity on the high seas and has so many variations it's tricky to find two made in the same way! The cocktail always reminds me of the Caribbean with its abundance of exotic ingredients and calm corners to chill out in. There's a particular beach on Sint Maarten where the waves lap around an old wooden jetty and the Yellowbirds flow like whispers on the breeze. With one of these on the go, it's your very own beachside moment – just close your eyes and you'll soon picture an awaiting hammock swaying under a Caribbean palm.

30ml (1oz) dark rum

30ml (1oz) three-year-old rum

15ml (½oz) banana liqueur

7.5ml (¼oz) Galliano

30ml (1oz) orange juice

22.5ml (¾oz) pineapple juice

7.5ml (¼oz) freshly squeezed lime juice

Ice: Cubed

Garnish: Pineapple wedge

Equipment: Cocktail shaker, strainer

Fill a shaker with ice

Add all the ingredients

Shake vigorously to chill

Strain into a glass filled with ice

Garnish with a pineapple wedge

CHICAGO FIZZ

Aaah, Chicago. I vividly remember visiting Rolling Meadows Brewery while filming in Illinois. It was a surreal day of epic adventure featuring drumming, poison ivy and a visit to the spot where Abraham Lincoln once worked as a ferryman on a bend in a river. Recuperating that evening after such high jinks back at my hotel bar in the Windy City, I raised several glasses of this marvellous drink in celebration. It seemed to me then, as it does now, that this is a very overlooked drink, and rather like the Chicago skyline, it will send your mood soaring. Port is too often associated with Christmas when in fact its quality demands it should be enjoyed all year round. Why on earth would you wait to enjoy something so splendid only once a year? And this cocktail is a great way to keep the port passing through your life. I'd stick with a young port, such as a ruby, for the primary fruit character and upbeat sweetness that dovetail with the rum. If you leave it to settle, the fine foam can always be topped up from the shaker. It's a drink of sculpture and structure as well as tasting sublime. I'm confident Abraham Lincoln would approve of its complexity and stature.

30ml (1oz) seven-year-old rum

30ml (1oz) port

15ml (½oz) freshly squeezed lemon juice

7.5ml (¼oz) simple syrup (see page 11)

½ an egg white

Soda water, to top

Ice: Cubed

Garnish: Lemon wheel

Equipment: Cocktail shaker, strainer

Dry shake all the ingredients except the soda water

Add ice to the shaker and shake to chill

Strain into a glass filled with ice and top with soda water

Garnish with a lemon wheel

Dry shaking = shaking without ice and then adding ice to chill. It helps the ingredients combine better, which is especially important when using egg whites.

Some people like to shake with ice first, then remove the ice and dry shake. This can be quite fiddly so I've kept it simple.

(See also my **Whisky Sour** recipes, page 228, for the same technique.)

ROSEMARY RUM SPRITZ

On my wedding day I was garnished with rosemary in my lapel instead of a flower. I'd read somewhere that rosemary is a symbol of remembrance and wanted to do a little something to honour those who couldn't be with us on that day, 7 September 2002. I like the aromatic edge of rosemary with red wine syrup: it's aromatic and complex rather than sticky and sweet and works splendidly to freshen up a spritz. It's spot-on to mark any special occasion, from anniversaries and family parties to celebrating brand new friendships!

45ml (1½oz) three-year-old rum

60ml (2oz) pink grapefruit juice

7.5ml (¼oz) red wine syrup (see page 11)

2 rosemary sprigs

Soda water, to top

Ice: Cubed

Garnish: Rosemary sprig

Equipment: Cocktail shaker, muddler and strainer

Muddle the rosemary in a shaker

Add ice and the remaining ingredients except the soda water

Shake vigorously to chill

Strain into a glass filled with ice and top with soda

Garnish with a sprig of rosemary

This is a really light and refreshing drink, not too sweet.

PIÑA COLADA

When I turned 18, I thought it would be cool to have a signature drink. I remember trying to order Piña Coladas in pubs and being stared at by faces that didn't so much say 'party' as 'shove off'. 'Piña Colada' is also the refrain of my wife Sophie in the small hours whenever a party is drawing to a close. The first time she bellowed this joyful phrase was in a small basement village bar in rural Spain on the eve of my forty-second birthday. To my amazement, the locals embraced the zeal and as my birthday dawned, we were all still at it. Piña Coladas are the home cocktail maker's shortcut to endurance. Let's look at it more carefully: pineapple juice and rum fleshed out with some citrus zing? Clearly those ingredients are fantastic at any time of the day – I'm talking 24-hour titillation. The thing about the Piña Colada is that it is a superbly classy drink that everybody mistakes for being in some way naff. I think partly this is because historically they've been made far too sweet and with not enough ice. And if you get the blending right to give that elusive balance and finesse, it manages to feel exotic and mellow with a discreet freshness and just enough tropical indulgence – as though someone has waved a wand at the sky to make it a little bit brighter.

60ml (2oz) three-year-old rum

30ml (1oz) pineapple juice

30ml (1oz) orange juice

22.5ml (¾oz) coconut cream

7.5ml (¼oz) freshly squeezed lime juice

Fresh pineapple slice (or tinned if you don't have fresh)

Ice: Crushed

Garnish: Fresh pineapple wedge (paper umbrella optional!)

Equipment: Blender

Place a scoop of crushed ice in a blender cup

Add all the ingredients

Blend until smooth

Tap into a piña or hurricane glass

Garnish with a pineapple wedge

WHISKY & BOURBON

Whisky is a mirror held up to sweet grain liquor canoodling with casks. The 'mash bill' of a whisky is the recipe of different grains used. In the case of single malt it'll be barley, which is the superstar of whisky grains. You can also find corn, which gives a certain sweetness (the recipe for bourbon is defined as having more than 51% corn), and then there's wheat and also rye. Rye gives a wonderful spicy tone – somewhere between cinnamon and nutmeg. Blending these together gives whiskies the basis of unique character. And it pays to pick a whisky you love for your cocktails. A reliable personal favourite blend of mine that you can track down easily worldwide is Johnnie Walker Black Label – it's sweet, rich and gently smoky. But choose your own favourite.

Time spent in wooden casks tutors the taste of whisky before it graduates into your glass. Casks that have previously held other drinks such as port, sherry or rum are used to 'finish' a whisky, giving extra nuance. And the area in which the whisky is made has a whopping impact, even on the spelling of the word: when it's made in Scotland it's always whisky. Whiskey with an 'e' tends to be American or Irish.

And remember, whisky is now made all over the world. Japanese whisky is particularly noteworthy and well worth exploring if you're after a dreamy dram. As for cocktails, it pays to get a grip on the terminology to lock on to the perfect flavour for the recipe you're making. I'd single out these three terms to enhance your creativity with cocktails.

Blended whisky/Scotch: The heart of whisky, blended from grain and single malt that's matured for more than three years in oak casks. The skill that goes into blending these is epic. Find your favourite brand and you'll be able to use it in most of the following cocktails.

Single malt: Always made from barley at an individual distillery in copper pot stills. Age in cask is indicated on the label. Scottish Speyside malts tend towards bright purity and are commonly matured in sherry casks; Islay malts are in the punchy, smokier bracket; Highland malts are diverse and drift towards the lighter side; Lowland malts are soft, light and smooth; Campbeltown's are as robust as the whole range of styles.

Bourbon: Must be made in the USA; around 95% is crafted in Kentucky. The mash bill has to be at least 51% corn and to qualify as 'straight' it has to be aged in new charred oak barrels for more than two years. Bourbon is whiskey, but not all whiskey is bourbon; its fruity, mellow tinge works superbly in summery drinks.

American rye whiskey: Must be made in the USA with at least 51% rye, which imbues cocktails with a spicy splendour.

Irish whiskey: Usually triple distilled, and must be made in Ireland then aged for at least three years in casks. Can be single malt, single grain, grain, blended or single pot still (a blend of both malted and unmalted barley), which is unique to Ireland. Irish whiskey brings a smooth, mellow magic to cocktails.

Most importantly, go exploring. With such diversity and calibre across the board, have fun finding the right bottle for your tastes.

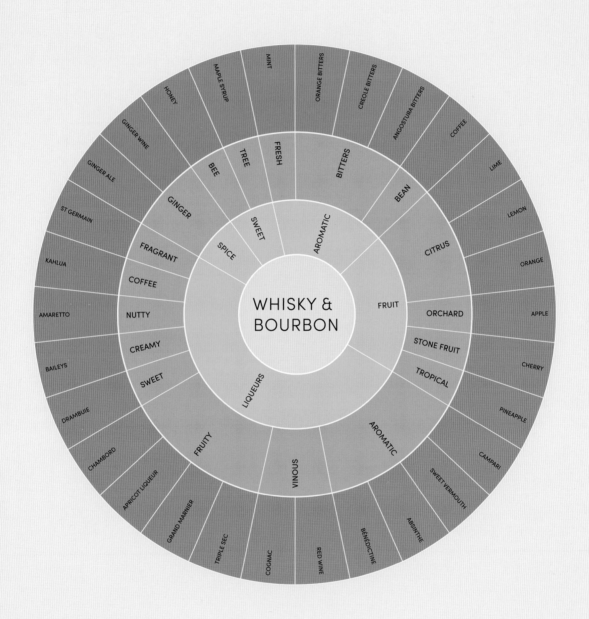

MINT JULEP

I've roared around Kentucky filming a documentary series about bourbon and I felt the hot thunder of hooves on the famous Derby racecourse of Churchill Downs. The speeding thrills combined well with a cool tin of condensation-covered Mint Julep in my happy hand. That's what this drink is all about – people coming together, refreshment on a hot day. It's an ice-cold format and nothing beats that tin cup to maintain shocking freshness. It's fundamentally a quenching drink, an invigorator, a nod to simplicity, standing for the prime rule of all cocktails: a sense of balance. I hold the Mint Julep in esteem – it's a pioneering early cocktail, an ancestor to the greats. This drink's got heritage as well as timeless presence thanks to the easy interplay of high-quality, precisely measured ingredients and that sweet, mellow, curling, spicy trail of bourbon threading the texture through diamonds of crushed ice. One scented breeze of Mint Julep invokes that feeling of high summertime in my garden – and you're all invited. It's green and buzzing, and you know what, all year round it makes me feel like I'm outdoors at a gently rising party with great friends.

60ml (2oz) bourbon

15ml (½oz) simple syrup (see page 11)

10 mint leaves

2 dashes Angostura Bitters

Ice: Crushed

Garnish: Mint sprig

Equipment: Muddler, long bar spoon

Muddle the mint leaves in a julep tin or glass

Pack with crushed ice

Add the remaining ingredients

Churn with a long bar spoon to mix

Cap with more crushed ice and garnish with a mint sprig

A traditional julep tin is usually used to make and serve this but any glass will do.

OLD FASHIONED

It's impossible to drink an Old Fashioned and not feel that you've stepped slightly deeper within yourself. Stretching back to the early 1800s, its roots linger through numerous variations woven through sweetness and an enduring burnished character that suggests low-lit, carefree dates and time to kill. I find it dreamy and reflective, the thickening texture of the sugar syrup expanding through that resonant, orangey bourbon and hypnotic amber trailing around a singular icy monolith. It's the equivalent of drinking what I imagine a bonfire would taste like if it was laced with demerara sugar and the well-wishes of all the fairies and gods hidden giggling in the shadows. Perhaps it's the echo of the charred oak that bourbon soaks into as it mellows and ages that brings this to the fore. I certainly love sipping an Old Fashioned at a barbecue. It stands for steadfast resolve – at a time when whisky cocktails became fancier and more convoluted, simple Old Fashioned cocktails held firm. The straightforward nature of the drink is, I suspect, what allows space for gentle sips to bring richer ideas to unpromising conversations, and the Old Fashioned strikes me as one of those rare cocktails where one is either too much or plenty. I witnessed this first-hand in the Pendennis Club in Louisville, Kentucky, which lays claim to the place where sugar syrup and muddled fruit first featured in the Old Fashioned. Who knows how much truth there is to this; all I can say for sure is that my drinking companion's appetite for the Old Fashioned was as undimmed as the dawn which crept imperceptibly around us as we continued gently chuckling into the rising light.

60ml (2oz) bourbon

7.5ml (¼oz) simple syrup (see page 11)

2 dashes Angostura Bitters

½ orange slice

½ lemon slice

1 maraschino cherry

Ice: Cubed

Garnish: Orange slice and cherry

Equipment: Muddler, long bar spoon

Muddle the orange, lemon and maraschino cherry in a glass

Use a long bar spoon to discard the fruit pulp

Add the bourbon, simple syrup and bitters

Stir gently to combine

Add ice (ideally one oversized cube)

Garnish with an orange slice and a cherry

For a sweeter, smokier drink swap the simple syrup for maple syrup.

This is traditionally made in the glass it's served in but you can also make it in a shaker then pour over ice.

MANHATTAN

One whisper of the word 'Manhattan' and New York instinctively pops up and packs the skyline of our minds. Tall, elegant buildings, firm sophistication and a frisson of social ruthlessness – this is a drink with classy presentation and vibrant colour, and it's always a hip-swing away from a riot of good times. It seems the drink was first shaken to life in New York around the 1880s, yet rather than investigating its origin, let's consider where it ended up. It's been around a long time, resurrected through various iterations, popular with the party set as well as erudites thanks to that union of spice and herbs through a prism of edgy fruit. It appears in the movie *Some Like It Hot*, it's soaked through the era of high kicks and padded shoulders and it's what we all want more of in our lives: Italian style in the hands of upstarts in America. And that's why I love the Manhattan. It's compact yet larger than life and always brings more impact than is strictly necessary.

60ml (2oz) bourbon

30ml (1oz) sweet vermouth

2 dashes Angostura Bitters

Ice: Cubed

Garnish: Speared cherry

Equipment: Cocktail shaker, long bar spoon, strainer

Fill a shaker with ice

Add all the ingredients

Stir well to chill

Strain into a chilled glass

Garnish with a speared cherry

For a **Dry Manhattan**, substitute sweet vermouth for dry. For a **Perfect Manhattan** add 15ml (½oz) each of sweet and dry vermouth.

RUSTY NAIL

This lovely cocktail is bafflingly underrated. Drambuie and Scotch come together in the Rusty Nail, the heart of Scotland: with sweet malt and spice, it's an elixir of generosity, an antidote to winter and the applause of summer. The Rusty Nail's fruit and spice on a sunny day tastes like a naughty, concentrated version of Pimm's. And in winter, it is the glowing equivalent of drinking the devil's soul – and in this case the devil is a lovely chap who wants to give you a cuddle. Maybe it's the words 'rust' and 'nail' in this cocktail's title that's been holding it back. Time for a rebrand? How about a 'Devil's Cuddle'? Who could resist!

45ml (1½oz) blended Scotch whisky

22.5ml (¾oz) Drambuie

Ice: Cubed

Garnish: Orange twist

Equipment: Cocktail shaker, strainer, long bar spoon

Fill a shaker with ice

Add all the ingredients

Stir well to chill

Strain into a glass filled with ice

Garnish with an orange twist

SAZERAC

I drank quite a few of these when visiting New Orleans. I'd just come from visiting the Buffalo Trace distillery, tucked in Kentucky between Lexington and Louisville. That's where Sazerac Straight Rye Whiskey is made, which thanks to the high rye content in the mash bill gives a spicy twist to the taste – a near-perfect spice-storm of pepper, aniseed and clove. Down in New Orleans at the Sazerac Coffee House on Royal Street, rye whiskey served with a dash of Peychaud's Bitters gave rise to the Sazerac, supposedly America's first branded cocktail. After a memorable day filming in locations that had previously been the backdrop to TV shows and movies from *Treme* to the James Bond film *Live and Let Die*, sipping my Sazerac made me feel both ready for an informal work meeting and set to impress a new drinking buddy with my upbeat exuberance. Sazerac is a discreet confidence booster and mood improver – I'm not saying you should rely on it, but you should certainly deploy it more regularly than you do.

60ml (2oz) American rye whiskey

7.5ml (¼oz) absinthe

7.5ml (¼oz) simple syrup (see page 11)

3 dashes Creole bitters

Ice: Cubed

Garnish: Lemon twist

Equipment: Cocktail shaker, long bar spoon, strainer

Pour the absinthe into a chilled glass, swill the liquid around and discard

Fill a shaker with ice and pour over the remaining ingredients

Stir gently to combine

Strain into the absinthe-rinsed glass

Garnish with a lemon twist

You can discard the absinthe into a shot glass and serve it as a chaser.

VIEUX CARRÉ

My first ever Vieux Carré was in New Orleans in the French Quarter just after I'd led a dancing parade down the street while filming an intro to a travel series. My legs felt the tornado of this drink slowly bringing them back to life. Got me right back on my feet, in fact, for jiggling the night away. This variation on the Manhattan was first served at the Hotel Monteleone's rotating Carousel Bar in the late 1930s by head bartender Walter Bergeron, and is pronounced 'Voo Carray' in the iconic spot where you can still order it today. The name translates to 'Old Square' or 'Old Quarter', a district of New Orleans now known as the French Quarter. I love it for its rare union of Cognac and bourbon, the grape and the grain flourishing within the scented splendour of Bénédictine's secret multiplicity of fragrant ingredients, fused with double bitters to whipcrack the blend away from cloying.

22.5ml (¾oz) bourbon

22.5ml (¾oz) Cognac

22.5ml (¾oz) sweet vermouth

7.5ml (¼oz) Bénédictine

2 dashes Creole bitters

1 dash Angostura Bitters

Ice: Cubed

Garnish: Lemon twist

Equipment: Cocktail shaker, long bar spoon, strainer

Fill a shaker with ice

Add all the ingredients

Stir well to chill

Strain into a glass filled with ice

Garnish with a lemon twist

NEW YORK SOUR

Apart from drinking it pure, this is the best use of red wine in the world. It takes the concept of blending red wine with fruit and hooks it up to the national grid. And while some cocktails are named after boroughs of New York – Manhattan, for instance – this cocktail takes the whole darn city and owns it. The triple titillation of a classic sour recipe – citrus with spirit and sugar – stretches back to 1862 with Jerry Thomas's famous *Bartenders Guide*. And mixing whiskey with wine isn't as odd as you might think – many whiskies are aged or 'finished' in casks that have previously held wine, fortified or otherwise, and the two have mysteriously harmonious interplay. The coolest thing about this cocktail, though, is its simplicity and knockout looks. It's fabulous to behold, delicious to indulge in and takes minimal time and effort. Satisfaction!

60ml (2oz) bourbon

22.5ml (¾oz) lemon juice

15ml (½oz) simple syrup (see page 11)

15ml (½oz) red wine

Ice: Cubed

Equipment: Cocktail shaker, long bar spoon, strainer

Fill a shaker with ice

Add all the ingredients except the wine and shake vigorously to chill

Strain into a glass filled with ice

Gently pour the wine into the drink over the back of a bar spoon so the wine floats on top

BOSTON SOUR

Invigoration in a glass! This takes the Whisky Sour to the next level with the silkification and fluffery of egg white (or aquafaba) delivering a svelte sense of smooth liquid ignition. All sours take you by the horns and lead you into the private party room. Inside you will find yourself tickled. I love all sours and with its luxuriant flourish, the Boston Sour ticks my box for a late-night tipple or summer patio sipper, or to while away your very next happy hour.

60ml (2oz) bourbon

22.5ml (¾oz) freshly squeezed lemon juice

15ml (½oz) simple syrup (see page 11)

½ an egg white

2 dashes Angostura Bitters

Ice: Cubed

Garnish: Lemon twist

Equipment: Cocktail shaker, strainer

Add all the ingredients to a shaker and shake to combine

Add ice and shake to chill

Strain into a chilled glass

Garnish with a lemon twist

Egg white can be substituted with 1 tbsp aquafaba.

Omit the egg white entirely if you want a classic **Whisky Sour**.

Substitute the simple syrup for the same amount of red wine syrup (see page 11) to create a hybrid **Boston/New York Sour**.

BOULEVARDIER

A little bit like a Negroni, but the gin is switched out for bourbon, which has earned this cocktail the nickname of Whisky Negroni. I prefer calling it a Depth Charge Negroni. The richer whisky gives the drink the weight and presence of all the best things in life – heavy-laid writing paper, bold velvet cushions and drifting into the settling calm of a massive soft armchair the size of a giant's glove. This is one of those cocktails of contemplation and if you're a fan of cigars, it can more than handle the woody, sweet, unfurling trail of steady scent. Alternatively, a good book will augment the mood just as well.

45ml (1½oz) bourbon

30ml (1oz) sweet vermouth

30ml (1oz) Campari

Ice: Cubed

Garnish: Orange twist

Equipment: Cocktail shaker, long bar spoon, strainer

Fill a shaker with ice

Add all the ingredients

Stir gently to combine

Strain into a chilled glass

Garnish with an orange twist

Essentially an **Autumnal Negroni**.

PENICILLIN

The answer to every ailment, imaginary or otherwise. With honey, lemon and ginger in this power pack, whether you feel a sniffle or not, the Penicillin should be sipped to keep the very thought of it at bay. The genius of this cocktail is the bedrock of sweet blended Scotch with that smoky tidal surge of peaty single malt whisky added at the end to cruise gently over the top of the drink. Add its jolt of lemon and scented ginger and this modern classic revives and sustains – think of it as the classiest way to recuperate after a hard day's toil.

60ml (2oz) blended whisky

22.5ml (¾oz) freshly squeezed lemon juice

22.5ml (¾oz) honey ginger syrup (see page 11)

7.5ml (¼oz) single malt whisky (anything with a peaty flavour profile works well)

Ice: Cubed

Garnish: Crystallised ginger

Equipment: Cocktail shaker, strainer, long bar spoon

Fill a shaker with ice

Add all the ingredients except the single malt whisky

Shake vigorously to chill

Strain into a glass filled with ice

Gently pour the single malt whisky into the drink over the back of a bar spoon so it floats on top

Garnish with crystallised ginger

The Penicillin was created by bartender Sam Ross as a contemporary twist on the classic **Gold Rush** (bourbon, lemon juice, honey syrup).

WHISKY PUNCH

Punches are there to be spiked – but in this case, there's no need! This recipe provides you a dynamic hit of perfectly balanced flavour to make your taste buds feel like they've gone interstellar. Gone are the days when punches were untended bowls of murky juice languishing in sports halls at regrettable civic events: think of this instead as a delicious alternative to the ubiquitous mojito.

45ml (1½oz) bourbon

22.5ml (¾oz) pineapple juice

22.5ml (¾oz) cloudy apple juice

7.5ml (¼oz) simple syrup (see page 11)

7.5ml (¼oz) freshly squeezed lime juice

6–8 mint leaves

30ml (1oz) soda water, to top

Ice: Cubed

Garnish: Mint sprig

Equipment: Muddler, cocktail shaker, strainer, long bar spoon

Muddle the mint leaves in a shaker

Fill the shaker with ice and add all the ingredients except the soda water

Shake vigorously to chill

Strain into a glass filled with ice and top with the soda water

Stir gently and garnish with a mint sprig

Light, refreshing and very easy to make.

GODFATHER

Almonds and Scotch. Sweetness and spice in one single sip. The glory of this drink is its simplicity and it's my all-time favourite nightcap. Mainly because rather than a second wind, it gives me a second breeze, which is ideal for listening to a few more tunes, having that last chat or just letting my mind unwind in poetry mode. You could use a single malt here, but I've always felt that's a bit like hiring James Gandolfini to star as a recalcitrant mob boss then asking him if he could play the part a bit more Oliver Hardy. Stick with what you've got – amaretto's interplay with the gentle, woody raisin flavours of a top blend is hard to beat. You could even say it's an offer you can't refuse. And why would you even try when the offer tastes this darn delicious?

60ml (2oz) blended Scotch whisky

15ml (½oz) amaretto

Ice: Cubed

Garnish: Orange twist and cherry

Equipment: Cocktail shaker, long bar spoon, strainer

Fill a shaker with ice

Add the Scotch and amaretto

Stir well to chill

Strain into a glass filled with ice

Garnish with an orange twist and a cherry

If you like your drink drier, add a little less amaretto.

Swap out the bourbon for vodka to make a **Godmother** – this is where you want to use a top-shelf vodka.

ROB ROY

Prepare for battle! Or, at least, for singing. I grew up roaming Stirlingshire during summers in Scotland with my Scottish granny regaling me with folk tales of Rob Roy and high adventure. The Rob Roy cocktail, while almost as full of character as the legendary Robert Roy MacGregor himself, was in fact created to honour the operetta of *Rob Roy* that was playing at New York's Herald Square Theatre in 1894. It's close to a Manhattan, with the difference of containing Scotch rather than American whiskey. And the difference is delicious. When I'm knocking up this drink, it always inspires me that it manages to highlight rather than obscure the ingredients and inevitably I end up casting my mind to the shores of Scotland, land of legends. After all, whatever inspires and endures has its roots in the unshakeable. And the warmth of my granny is a rock that always stands proudly in my heart.

60ml (2oz) blended Scotch whisky

30ml (1oz) sweet vermouth

2 dashes Angostura Bitters

Ice: Cubed

Garnish: Orange twist and cherry

Equipment: Cocktail shaker, strainer

Fill a shaker with ice

Add all the ingredients

Stir well to chill

Strain into a glass filled with ice

Garnish with an orange twist and a cherry

WHISKY MAC

My grandfather's favourite drink was the Whisky Mac. I noted that he would drink it during the rugby, he would drink it before lunch, he would drink it after breakfast, and he would also drink it before bed. I think my grandfather lived off Whisky Mac and would often say with assumed confidence that he didn't think there was any alcohol in green ginger wine. I don't think we need to worry whether we believe him or not, I just think we need to agree that this was among his many eccentric routines that kept him alive well into his eighties.

45ml (1½oz) blended Scotch whisky

30ml (1oz) Stones Green Ginger Wine

Ice: Cubed

Equipment: Cocktail shaker, long bar spoon, strainer

Fill a shaker with ice

Add all the ingredients

Stir well to chill

Strain into a glass filled with ice

Swap out the Scotch for a white rum to make a **Stone & Gravel**. Gin is also a good alternative.

HIGHLAND HEDGEROW

I love the hedgerow! So much so that I built a viewing platform in my garden – affectionately nicknamed the Poop Deck – to bring aperitifs eye-height with the hedgerow at the bottom of my garden. It's lovely to be able to pick blackberries from a deckchair but my real thrill comes earlier in the season, watching butterflies and bees pollinating all the wild flowers wreathed through the hedge. Fragrant and fruity, this cocktail will guide you effortlessly to the very heart of nature's highway. Raspberries ripple through Chambord and charmingly elide with the zingy apple juice. Apricots and elderflower caress the scent of the cocktail and by the time you've sipped one you'll feel like you're right up next to me on the Poop Deck peering at the flowers forming into fruit.

37.5ml (1¼oz) blended Scotch whisky

22.5ml (¾oz) Chambord

7.5ml (¼oz) apricot liqueur

7.5ml (¼oz) St-Germain elderflower liqueur

75ml (2½oz) cloudy apple juice

Ice: Cubed

Garnish: Skewered blackberry and raspberry

Equipment: Cocktail shaker, strainer

Fill a shaker with ice

Add all the ingredients

Shake vigorously to chill

Strain into a glass filled with ice

Garnish with a skewered blackberry and raspberry

AGGRAVATION

Working at the Cameo Cinema in Edinburgh's Tollcross as a student, I loved the atmosphere, the movies – and the free popcorn. One of the first movies I watched on the day I was promoted from snack seller to box office was *The Big Lebowski* in which Jeff Bridges sank creamy White Russians with a combination of leisurely elan and insouciant languor that still inspires me into relaxation to this day. The Aggravation adds a touch of jet propulsion to that mood thanks to the sweetness and spice of the whisky. The irony of this drink is that it comes without aggravation and settles you into a splendid wave of tranquil equanimity that even life's most determined ripples can't disturb. At ease!

45ml (1½oz) blended Scotch whisky

22.5ml (¾oz) Kahlua

30ml (1oz) single (light) cream

7.5ml (¼oz) simple syrup (see page 11)

Ice: Cubed

Garnish: Grated nutmeg

Equipment: Cocktail shaker, strainer

Fill a shaker with ice

Add all the ingredients

Shake vigorously to chill

Strain into a glass filled with ice

Garnish with grated nutmeg

PRESBYTERIAN

Refreshing and light as surfing the bubbles from a cascade of good cheer. This is a great summer sipper. One of my favourite drinks in the world is Scotch and soda – with the addition of a little squirt of ginger ale that beautifully boosts the sweet barley of the Scotch. These are drinks that are appropriate in my view before seeing a gig – they supply just the right amount of booze to give you the mood-enhancing focus required to meld with the music. Just ask Mark Lanegan: I had a few of these before a gig of his at the Roundhouse in London and he seemed to love my spirited spontaneous backing vocals.

45ml (1½oz) blended Scotch whisky

45ml (1½oz) soda water, to top

30ml (1oz) ginger ale, to top

Ice: Cubed

Garnish: Lemon wedge

Equipment: Long bar spoon

Fill a glass with ice

Pour in the whisky

Top with the soda water and ginger ale

Stir gently to combine

Garnish with a lemon wedge

ALGONQUIN

Rye whiskey, vermouth, pineapple juice? This, on paper, sounds like madness! Like invisible architecture. And yet when you sip it, this cocktail has all the presence and gravity-defying splendour of the Eiffel Tower. The sturdy Algonquin Hotel in New York, where this cocktail is supposed to have been created, has been standing near Times Square since 1902 and is designated a Historic Landmark. The hotel hosted the famous Algonquin Round Table of creatives, including Dorothy Parker and Harpo Marx, who met for lunch in the main dining room almost daily for a decade. The *New Yorker* magazine emerged from the literary set at these get-togethers and is, to this day, given free to all the guests at the Algonquin. I'd love the hotel even more if they gave everyone a free daily cocktail! But perhaps that's as absurd as invisible architecture.

45ml (1½oz) American rye whiskey

22.5ml (¾oz) sweet vermouth

22.5ml (¾oz) pineapple juice

2 dashes Angostura Bitters

Ice: Cubed

Garnish: Pineapple wedge

Equipment: Cocktail shaker, strainer

Fill a shaker with ice

Add all the ingredients

Stir well to chill

Strain into a chilled glass

Garnish with a pineapple wedge

LYNCHBURG LEMONADE

This is a cocktail famously made with Jack Daniel's, but any other Tennessee whiskey will do. There are strict rules around drinking in Lynchburg, Tennessee. You can't buy hard liquor there. It's illegal. Moore County, home to the Jack Daniel's distillery, has remained 'dry' since Prohibition. Thankfully, when I visited with master distiller Jeff Arnett, thanks to the nature of our 'work' I was able to sample a good deal of the gold flowing from his tasty treasury. I was fascinated to see the inferno as sugar maple is made into charcoal on site, which the spirit is gently filtered through to mellow for three to five days. And the barrel-ageing process is like a cross between Jenga and chess in the barrelhouse. Barrels on the upper floors tend to mature more quickly because it's warmer, so the job of the master distiller is to keep an eye on them all – to maintain a seamless final blend takes considerable skill. I like to think of this cocktail as a reward for all that hard work: Jack Daniel's loves being paired with orangey flavours and here the citrus refreshment takes the whole experience to a deep summery explosion of liquid splendour. And if you're sipping these at a barbecue, a chargrilled lemon wedge makes a delicious garnish. Ooooh, invite me round.

22.5ml (¾oz) Jack Daniel's or Tennessee whiskey

22.5ml (¾oz) triple sec

45ml (1½oz) lemon-lime soda*

30ml (1oz) freshly squeezed lemon juice

Ice: Cubed

Garnish: Lemon wedge

Equipment: Cocktail shaker, strainer

Fill a shaker with ice

Add all the ingredients except the lemon-lime soda

Shake vigorously to chill

Strain into glass filled with ice

Top with lemon-lime soda and garnish with a lemon wedge

*Lemon-lime soda = Sprite/7 Up.

IRISH COFFEE

I always look forward to an Irish Coffee – the indulgence of cream poured over the back of a spoon is a silky, floating treat. My wife Sophie loves it for the sweet, boozy kick. In fact, one memorable evening out, I remember she nearly chewed the caramel rim of her glass off (alarmingly, including the glass), such was the level of her delight – a few gentle words of restraint and a second Irish Coffee saved the day. My in-laws live on the west coast of Ireland in Ballyferriter, not far from Dingle. The best Irish Coffees in my experience come at unexpected moments – yes, I am explicitly saying that this is not just an after-dinner drink. Off on a cold winter's walk? This is a virtual sock of love around your wiggling toes. Summer in the garden? Irish Coffee time. I've had great times down the pub with this concoction and that warm, bubbling mood is so easy – and quick – to evoke at home with this wonderful drink that for years got stuck at the end of dinner. Time to make this Irish Coffee your headline event.

30ml (1oz) Irish whiskey

15ml (½oz) Baileys

15ml (½oz) simple syrup (see page 11)

Freshly brewed coffee

Garnish: Double (heavy) cream and a coffee bean

Equipment: Long bar spoon

Pour the whiskey, Baileys and syrup into a mug

Fill to three-quarters with freshly brewed coffee and stir

Float double cream on top and garnish with a coffee bean

COBBLER

Who knew that whisky could be so refreshing! This cocktail tastes like a citrus grove infused with an exotic tropical breeze. I remember horse riding through a South American vineyard with Madame Marnier herself – yes, Marnier as in the family who came up with the orangey elixir in this recipe. She was so charming and beyond formidable that I remember thinking her horse never stood a chance. Even after she appraised my unorthodox and altogether gentler approach to riding (sit and pray) I was nonetheless treated to a spectacular feast overlooking Chile's Colchagua Valley. I admit, it's a little hazy now, but I could swear we ended up knocking back Cobblers and laughing into the cool night air. I think at one point I even agreed to take part in the Dakar Rally with Madame Marnier's son. An excellent reflection of this drink's horizon-expanding prowess.

45ml (1½oz) blended Scotch whisky

22.5ml (¾oz) Grand Marnier

7.5ml (¼oz) freshly squeezed lemon juice

7.5ml (¼oz) simple syrup (see page 11)

½ an orange slice

Small pineapple slice

Ice: Cubed

Garnish: Orange twist

Equipment: Cocktail shaker, strainer

Muddle the fruit in a shaker

Fill with ice and add the remaining ingredients

Shake vigorously to chill

Strain into a chilled glass

Garnish with an orange twist

APPLE WHISKY

There are two things you need to know about me: one is never enough, and two, I think apple blossom is the finest scent. I'd pitch it against any rose and I love it for its delicacy, high finesse and fleeting magic. Gone in a week, it's so subtle – you really have to bullseye your nose right in the middle of the tiny flower's dartboard to get a good whiff. And the blossom is doubly special thanks to the fruit it bears, transforming into the apples we see commonly and always fail to appreciate fully. Think of all the varieties – and I urge you to experiment with unique local juices in this recipe to make it your own. Jonagold, Pink Lady, Cox... their subtleties are endless. I particularly love the sweetness of Egremont Russet juice – hunt it down. Ah, that blossom: I etch it in my diary to take three days off and revel in the delicate, breezy dance of the orchard's scent. Once a year is never enough for me, and this cocktail lets me wend any time back through the orchard to give my regards to the trees and find myself sipping the juice of the apple and the lost dream of the bloom.

45ml (1½oz) bourbon

75ml (2½oz) cloudy apple juice

15ml (½oz) maple syrup

15ml (½oz) freshly squeezed lemon juice

2 dashes orange bitters

Ice: Cubed

Garnish: Apple slice

Equipment: Cocktail shaker, long bar spoon, strainer

Fill a shaker with ice

Add all the ingredients

Stir gently to chill

Strain into a chilled glass

Garnish with a slice of apple

CRANACHAN

A pudding in a cocktail. That's like a simultaneous disco-blast of the verse and chorus of Dancing Queen. Double Abba? What's not to love? Inspiring indulgence with a creamy conundrum, this is a great alternative to a Bloody Mary on a Sunday morning. Sure, it's at the other end of the flavour spectrum – and that's the glory of it. I had a great-aunt called Betty, and while she wasn't cruising around in her perambulator, according to legend she would take her porridge with a little bit of honey, a sprinkle of raspberries from the garden and heroic lashings of whisky smuggled aboard. Delicious, and this cocktail would, I'm sure, have Auntie Betty up and at it in the kitchen disco listening to double Abba. AABBBBAA!

37.5ml (1¼oz) whisky

15ml (½oz) Chambord

60ml (2oz) single (light) cream

15ml (½oz) honey

6 raspberries

Ice: Cubed

Garnish: Toasted oats

Equipment: Muddler, cocktail shaker and strainer

Muddle the raspberries in a shaker

Add ice to the muddled raspberries along with the remaining ingredients

Shake vigorously until the shaker is frosted

Strain into a chilled glass

Garnish with a sprinkle of toasted oats

BACK OF THE CUPBOARD & SPECIALITY

Sometimes the best things in life are lurking in the shadows. This section of the book is the torch for you to cast light on to the mysterious bottles that have lain undisturbed like the ancient rulers of a nether realm at the back of your cupboard.

There's always a route into a cocktail from the most unlikely source – I'm thinking oddly shaped bottles, lurid liqueurs and those barely touched beauties that we're never quite sure when to pour. Let these receptacles of rough magic encourage us into uncharted concoctions of daring simplicity.

There's no getting away from it – some of these bottles contain flavours and fragrances so potent and curious that blending them is the golden key to unlock their hidden charms. In these easily assembled drinks, such rogue libations are tamed into bringing more character than quirk.

So be brave, dust down these peculiar potions and let's send them beyond the very frontier of flavour.

JAPANESE SLIPPER

In the 1980s I toured Japan as a singer, around the same time as this cocktail was created. I remember very distinctly looking out over Mount Fuji at dawn: the lakes of cloud, the air pristine as a petal, a paper door opening onto a world of eerie green lightness. All these years later, that moment inspired me to make my version of this classic cocktail. The mellow fragrance of Midori, the bright, sunlit clarity of lemon juice with the joyful citrus caress of Cointreau. There's something of the sweet serenity of that moment in this simple modern classic. May your Japanese Slipper fit a perfectly magical moment for you.

22.5ml (¾oz) Cointreau

22.5ml (¾oz) Midori

22.5ml (¾oz) freshly squeezed lemon juice

Ice: Cubed

Garnish: Speared maraschino cherry

Equipment: Cocktail shaker, strainer

Fill a shaker with ice

Add all the ingredients

Shake vigorously to chill

Strain into a chilled glass

Garnish with a speared maraschino cherry

ALABAMA SLAMMER

I am a servant of sloes – I pick them from the blackthorn bushes at the bottom of my garden next to my viewing platform I have dubbed the 'Poop Deck'. My family all thought I'd lost the plot when I built a platform as high as the hedge overlooking a field of sheep. Partly I did it for the view, but also to gain access to the elusive higher sloes on the giant blackthorn, which is known as Goliath. I have a library of aged sloe gins from down the decades, and while some reveal hidden layers of sumptuous, spicy evolution, for this recipe the most youthful, vibrant sloe gin is required for the full fruity impact. The name for this cocktail is said to have emerged from the University of Alabama in the late 20th century, but my version emerged as I was dozing on the Poop Deck admiring the beard of blossom on Goliath and casting my mind forward to the coming crop of sloes.

22.5ml (¾oz) sloe gin

22.5ml (¾oz) Southern Comfort

22.5ml (¾oz) amaretto

60ml (2oz) freshly squeezed orange juice

7.5ml (¼oz) freshly squeezed lemon juice

Ice: Cubed

Garnish: Orange slice and cherry

Equipment: Cocktail shaker, strainer

Fill a shaker with ice

Add all the ingredients

Shake vigorously to chill

Strain into a glass filled with ice

Garnish with a slice of orange and a cherry

BALTIMORE ZOO

This is a serious drink, with six spirits topped with beer. Everything but the kitchen sink goes in: it's a true back-of-the-cupboard classic.

Its ingredients come from all over the world. They form a heady concoction, and a day off with a daring companion is a perfect opportunity to create this pokey drink. If you're a fan of powerful classics like the Long Island Iced Tea, you'll love a trip to Baltimore Zoo. This drink is a visitor attraction in its own right: fortunately, once you've served it, the price of admission is free.

15ml (½oz) amaretto

15ml (½oz) peach schnapps

15ml (½oz) three-year-old rum

15ml (½oz) vodka

15ml (½oz) gin

15ml (½oz) triple sec

30ml (1oz) freshly squeezed lemon juice

7.5ml (¼oz) grenadine

Beer, to top

Ice: Cubed

Garnish: Lemon wedge

Equipment: Cocktail shaker, strainer

Fill a shaker with ice

Add all the ingredients except the beer

Shake vigorously to chill

Strain into a glass filled with ice and top with beer

Garnish with a lemon wedge

AMARETTO SOUR

During a particularly ferocious winter living on Edinburgh's Bernard Terrace, amaretto was my drink of choice for many months. Perhaps it was the sweet, sustaining simplicity, or maybe I was in a particularly 'almond' frame of mind. My curiosity with cocktails led me to the Amaretto Sour, and I realised just how sublime the Italian liqueur that gives it its name can be. It has a syrupy sweet twist to it, but here the lemon juice turns the ignition and accelerates through the cherry bitters – and it's all laced with the luxuriance of egg white. For me, the Amaretto Sour reminds me of experiments in Edinburgh. For you, wherever you're making it, rest assured: this is a potion poured directly from the laboratory of loveliness and is a steadfast stunner.

60ml (2oz) amaretto

30ml (1oz) freshly squeezed lemon juice

½ an egg white

Dash cherry bitters (optional)

Ice: Cubed

Garnish: Lemon twist and cherry

Equipment: Cocktail shaker, strainer

Add all the ingredients to a shaker and dry shake (see page 211) to combine

Fill the shaker with ice

Shake vigorously to chill

Strain into a glass filled with ice

Garnish with a lemon twist and a cherry

THE
GREEN DREAM

I designed this because I had some soju at the back of my cupboard and was wondering what to do with it. This curious Korean spirit has an appley taste, which drew me immediately to Monin Pomme Verte. Freshly squeezed lemon juice brightens and soda water refreshes: it's a massive delight to drink. You could make it in pitchers to serve to your friends, and for me it is the ultimate cocktail to sip on a hot day, as unexpected as a board meeting hosted by Iron Man, entertaining as Aretha Franklin in full flight and as joyful as a chorus of happy partygoers raising their glasses to the good times.

45ml (1½oz) soju

15ml (½oz) Monin Pomme Verte

7.5 ml (¼oz) freshly squeezed lemon juice

45ml (1½oz) soda water, to top

Ice: Cubed

Garnish: Apple slice

Equipment: Long bar spoon

Fill a glass with ice

Add all the ingredients except the soda water

Top with the soda water

Stir gently to combine

Garnish with a slice of apple

A perfect summer-evening barbecue cocktail and easy to scale up to serve in batches.

BOSTON
TEA PARTY

My friend Krisna made me a version of this cocktail after he had a stint living in Boston as a lobster fisherman. He said it was inspired by the sea spray, although I think he was just freezing cold and this drink was the perfect tonic to unthaw his frosty fisherman's fingers. This drink may look a little like tea but the presence of coffee in its flavour is indisputable. The American War of Independence famously followed in the wake of the Boston Tea Party protest on 16 December 1773 when a shipment of tea was destroyed in Boston harbour. Events, like flavours, can be as unpredictable as they are momentous. And this drink is as monumental as a cocktail can be.

15ml (½oz) Grand Marnier

15ml (½oz) Tia Maria

15ml (½oz) three-year-old rum

15ml (½oz) vodka

15ml (½oz) gin

15ml (½oz) triple sec

30ml (1oz) freshly squeezed lemon juice

7.5ml (¼oz) simple syrup (see page 11)

Cola, to top

Ice: Cubed

Garnish: Lemon wedge

Equipment: Cocktail shaker, strainer

Fill a shaker with ice

Add all the ingredients except the cola

Shake vigorously to chill

Strain into a glass filled with ice and top with cola

Garnish with a lemon wedge

MOON PULSE

As you drink this, the ice cream moon melts down through the drink. It's very rich and creamy. You'll need a straw (reusable please) to manage it.

I designed the Moon Pulse to be a riff on a White Russian, with a dose more vanilla and ice cream to evoke that holiday feeling. Yes, I love a float, and the cool vanilla orb in this cocktail sort of reminds me of the moon. I adore cold, creamy drinks as much as I love creating them, and this is a tribute to the power of the Moon, the bouncing beams of light and the shadows it casts. It's a strange, spherical body that rises every night; we occasionally catch sight of it and it deserves to be celebrated in a drink. The Moon pulls the tides, encourages the rising of sap and controls the rhythm of the seasons. It's time to take its pulse and gratefully appreciate its steady beat.

45ml (1½oz) vanilla vodka

15ml (½oz) Kahlua

15ml (½oz) Frangelico

60ml (2oz) single (light) cream

1 scoop vanilla ice cream

Ice: Cubed

Equipment: Cocktail shaker, strainer

Fill a shaker with ice

Add all the ingredients except the ice cream

Shake vigorously to chill

Strain into a glass three-quarters filled with ice

Float the ball of ice cream on top

TOASTED ALMOND

A deluxe, divine alternative to dessert. It's well worth blending this until it becomes a silky, cooling, after-dinner indulgence. I always feel inspired to make a Toasted Almond to reflect my love of the affogato (coffee splashed over a scoop of vanilla ice cream, often with a crunchy biscuit tossed in). Honed over many iterations, this is the recipe that proves once and for all that the Toasted Almond is, in my view, the greatest pudding of all time.

30ml (1oz) Disaronno amaretto

30ml (1oz) Kahlua

2 scoops vanilla ice cream

Small handful crushed ice

Ice: Crushed

Garnish: Spray cream

Equipment: Blender

Add all the ingredients to a blender cup along with a small handful of crushed ice

Blend until smooth

Pour the mixture into a glass – you'll need to give it a good tap to get it moving

Garnish with a swirl of spray cream

JELLY BEAN

Jelly beans, in my experience, have been known to assuage the symptoms of a hangover – or 'wearing the Helmet of Thunder' as I like to call it. This is a drink that also has a certain reviving impact. With the aniseed of the Pernod, the juicy, black fruit of the crème de mûre, and the sweet and sharp blended juice and syrup, I'd say this is one for the cocktail connoisseur. If you're seeking to impress, craft this, hand it to your guests and stand well back. It's either going to go one way or the other, but one thing everyone can agree on is how marvellous the colour is – it just needs 'Purple Rain' as a soundtrack.

30ml (1oz) Pernod

30ml (1oz) crème de mûre

22.5ml (¾oz) freshly squeezed lemon juice

15ml (½oz) freshly squeezed lime juice

7.5ml (¼oz) simple syrup (see page 11)

Ice: Cubed

Garnish: Lime wheel, and jelly beans on the side

Equipment: Cocktail shaker, strainer

Fill a shaker with ice

Add all the ingredients

Shake vigorously to chill

Strain into a chilled glass

Garnish with a lime wheel and a side of jelly beans to eat while you drink

If you want to achieve the full bright purple effect, buy the brightest and most lurid crème de mûre you can find!

FROZEN GRASSHOPPER

The Grasshopper is a drink as iconic as the BMX bike, the Eiffel Tower or the very thought of a snoozing koala bear. Fortunately, my Frozen Grasshopper is instantly available to all with a little ingenuity and appreciation of the finer things in life. Clearly, I am referring here to both crème de menthe and crème de cacao. I can see you considering turning your nose up at these fine ingredients, but I urge you to turn your nose the other way into their wonderful aromas, irresistible textures and sumptuous, enveloping admirability. As at home on the ski slopes as it is on a beach in summer, the Frozen Grasshopper is quite simply a minty hoot – have some fun with it.

30ml (1oz) green crème de menthe

30ml (1oz) white crème de cacao

2 scoops vanilla ice cream

Ice: Crushed

Garnish: Chocolate powder

Equipment: Blender

Add all the ingredients to a blender cup along with a small handful of crushed ice

Blend until smooth

Pour the mixture into a glass – you'll need to give it a good tap to get it moving

Garnish with a light dusting of chocolate powder

In essence this is a very grown-up version of mint choc-chip ice cream.

To make a classic **Grasshopper**, omit the ice cream and substitute with 2 tbsp single (light) cream. Shake the ingredients over ice and strain into a Y-shaped glass.

CHOCONANA

My first frozen banana drink was in Jalan Jaksa, Jakarta, when I realised my whole life munching bananas had been a mere precursor to drinking them. Why nibble when you can sip? Inspired to lengthen and extend the banana, I came up with this recipe in homage to diner desserts and proud puddings, to every cocktail that before becoming a classic was considered a little 'out there'. Behold my Choconana: it's utterly scrumptious.

30ml (1oz) crème de banane

15ml (½oz) dark crème de cacao

2 scoops vanilla ice cream

¼ of a fresh banana

15ml (½oz) chocolate sauce

Ice: Crushed

Garnish: Banana slice and chocolate sauce

Equipment: Blender

Add all the ingredients to a blender cup along with a small handful of crushed ice

Blend until smooth

Pour the mixture into a glass – you'll need to give it a good tap to get it moving

Garnish with a slice of banana and a little more chocolate sauce

BANANA SPLIT

When going out for a meal in the early 1980s, the banana split was the height of exotic desserts, perhaps rivalled only by the Dusty Road and the Knickerbocker Glory. The greatest banana splits always have the full whack of sauces, ice cream and sprinkles. I've tried to bring all that satisfying complexity to this drink by using crème de cacao as well as crème de banane and fraise, fresh fruit, ice cream and sticky chocolate sauce. It's something of a trip down memory lane, this drink, to a land of long spoons and glass bowls and holding back the urge to lick them clean. In this case, if your tongue is long enough, I would salute you if it can reach the bottom of the glass. That's how good this cocktail really is.

15ml (½oz) crème de banane

15ml (½oz) dark crème de cacao

15ml (½oz) crème de fraise

¼ of a fresh banana

15ml (½oz) strawberry purée

15ml (½oz) chocolate sauce

2 scoops vanilla ice cream

Ice: Crushed

Garnish: A strawberry, banana slice and chocolate sauce

Equipment: Blender

Add all the ingredients to a blender cup along with a small handful of crushed ice

Blend until smooth

Pour the mixture into a glass – you'll need to give it a good tap to get it moving

Garnish with a strawberry, a slice of banana and a little more chocolate sauce

STRAWBERRY SHORTCAKE

Sometimes the liquid version of a dessert is even better than the real thing, and my Strawberry Shortcake is hard to beat. I love it with afternoon tea, scones, cream and jam, the sound of birdsong and my family merrily murmuring around me. Make it for your moment, and whether you're serving it for a sweet treat, an after-dinner delight or just someone you love, give yourself a pat on the back. You've made the effort and it's well worth it.

30ml (1oz) crème de fraise

30ml (1oz) amaretto

2 scoops vanilla ice cream

Ice: Crushed

Garnish: Whipped cream and a strawberry

Equipment: Blender

Add all the ingredients to a blender cup along with a small handful of crushed ice

Blend until smooth

Pour the mixture into a glass – you'll need to give it a good tap to get it moving

Garnish with a swirl of whipped cream and a strawberry

CALYPSO

This cocktail is a dance, a dream of the nymph Calypso who was said to have entranced Odysseus on her magical island for seven years. Exotic and far-flung flavours combine in a spirited tribute to the tantalising, tropical, mellow magic brought by all of these ingredients. The inspiration for this cocktail was my time spent in the Turks and Caicos islands. I was avoiding a tidal flood, and as I waded away from danger holding my luggage aloft, I vowed I would create a cocktail to give thanks for escaping to the island's interior. So this drink is in honour of both Calypso the nymph and my healthy respect for the ocean – and gratitude for a well-stocked bar after a narrow escape.

22.5ml (¾oz) coconut rum (e.g. Malibu)

15ml (½oz) mango liqueur

15ml (½oz) passion fruit liqueur

15ml (½oz) mango purée

2 scoops vanilla ice cream

Ice: Crushed

Garnish: Shaved coconut and mango slice

Equipment: Blender

Add all the ingredients to a blender cup along with a small handful of crushed ice

Blend until smooth

Pour the mixture into a glass – you'll need to give it a good tap to get it moving

Garnish with a sprinkle of shaved coconut and a slice of mango

WINE

From fortified to fizz, wine is a world of flavours, textures and intensities offering endless excellent permutations for creating cocktails. With a stack of different origins, ages and expressions, my rule of thumb with mixing wine is to stick to a good level of quality without blowing the bank. Just bear in mind that if you're pouring something that doesn't suit your palate in the first place, the subsequent cocktail is unlikely to be to your taste either, so choose wines you love to base these recipes on. Southern French reds, Italian whites, Spanish bargains and Chilean wine in general are all good places to rummage. I'd steer clear of any wines that are aged and savoury (stick to those under a year or two old), as these cocktails all benefit from youthful, fruity vigour.

Wine in its myriad forms has been a constant delight in my life. While there are some who believe that wine is inherently sacred and must never be blended beyond its own bottling, I am a huge fan of simple wine-based cocktails – White Port and Tonic, for instance, garnished with a citrus slice, is a simple and delicious alternative to a G&T. There's really no reason that wine shouldn't feature as a headline ingredient in gorgeous cocktails. As long as the quality of its character is balanced with complementing or contrasting flavours, I say let's have fun and amplify the world of wine even more widely.

I feel sure Bacchus himself would approve – after all, the god of wine loves a party. And as you sip these cocktails in the spirit of good times, raise your glass and rally the moment with my motto – All For Wine And Wine For All!

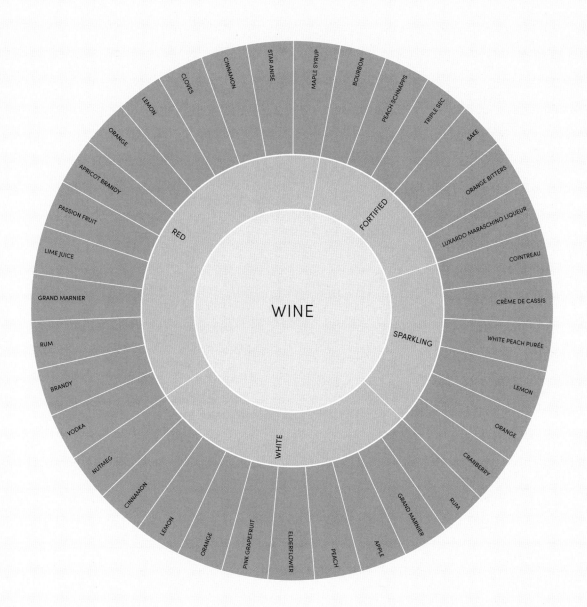

WINE

KIR ROYALE

For many years, my parents were obsessed with sparkling wine from Saumur. They became so entranced with the chateaux of the Loire and the vineyards flanking this noble wine river that they journeyed there for many years in search of the source of the Loire. There is in fact a photograph of my parents sitting next to a trickle of muddy water which they insist is the beginning of all that is born on the shoulders of that rolling, living highway to the Atlantic. The sparkling Saumur wine they brought home in pristine white boxes was always customised into their favourite cocktail at the time, the Kir Royale. It was a Sunday tradition in my household. My father was a teacher, my mother was a nurse, and this was their luxurious escape into one another's arms before feeding their family. While I'm delighted to recommend using Champagne in this recipe, in honour of my mum and dad, I urge you to try the splendour of Saumur, with its bright, fruity briskness.

15ml (½oz) crème de cassis

Champagne or sparkling wine, to top

Garnish: Seasonal berries

Pour the crème de cassis into a flute

Drop the seasonal berry garnish into the drink

Top with Champagne (or sparkling wine)

This works nicely with a good sparkling cider instead of Champagne.

To make a **Kir** just swap Champagne for a dry white wine. You don't need to use your best wine for this, in fact it's a good way of using up a wine that may not be to your taste.

You can try red wine instead of white to make a **Cardinal**.

MIMOSA

A drink of legends stretching back to Paris in the 1920s, the Mimosa is a drink most of us are familiar with from knocking orange juice into sparkling wine on Christmas morning. The Mimosa's magic comes from its equilibrium, which is precisely measured. It is also a drink of time travel: you'll notice your first sip, but you'll probably next notice when your glass is empty and needs refreshing. That doesn't mean the drink is ineffective; on the contrary, the drink has delivered you to where you always ought to have been – in the company of others and focused on having fun. Cheers!

90ml (3oz) Champagne

90ml (3oz) freshly squeezed orange juice

Ice: Cubed

Garnish: Orange slice

Fill a wine glass two-thirds with ice

Pour the Champagne over the ice

Top with the orange juice

Garnish with a slice of orange

To make a **Bucks Fizz**, omit the ice and serve two parts Champagne to one part orange juice.

Pour 1 tbsp of Grand Marnier over the top to make a **Grand Mimosa**.

Both the Bucks Fizz and the Mimosa are overdue a revival: they've been given a bad name thanks to being served lukewarm or with cheap, cartoned orange juice. But use good-quality fizz and freshly squeezed juice and you can't go wrong.

WHITE PEACH BELLINI

One summer, while living on the island of Jersey, I became entranced with peach schnapps. I would top it up with lemonade, and it fuelled a headily memorable summer which I nicknamed 'Destination Discotheque'. The first time I heard the whisper of a Bellini that year I began building a rocket in my mind to explore the heavens in search of Planet Peach. The drink originated in Harry's Bar in Venice, where it was famously created by Giuseppe Cipriani. I fled to Venice while fresh peaches were in season in search of the greatest recipe. While I love the local Italian prosecco in a classic Bellini for the mellow, fruity freshness, if you switch it out for Champagne, there's a little more zing in the mix, which works a charm with the enhanced sweet character of white peaches.

30ml (1oz) white peach purée

15ml (½oz) peach schnapps

7.5ml (¼oz) freshly squeezed lemon juice

75ml (2½oz) Champagne, to top

Ice: Cubed

Garnish: Peach slice

Equipment: Cocktail shaker, strainer

Fill a shaker with ice

Add all the Ingredients except the Champagne

Shake vigorously to chill

Pour the fizz into a chilled glass

Strain the shaken mixture over the bubbles

Garnish with a peach slice

Swap the Champagne for soda water to make a **Peach Fizz**.

The purée can make the drink froth so pour carefully.

And the options for the purée are endless, with lots of opportunities to experiment. But if you're going to make your own, take the skin off the peaches first. If you can't find white peach purée, normal peaches or nectarines will work too.

CREOLE LADY

The island of Madeira is one of my favourite
drinks destinations. I like to sit in the town
as butterflies flit around the banana trees,
surrounded by the floral cascade and the
hot scent of the sea. Madeira is an island of
intoxicating character. The local fortified
wines are marked by their natural acidity.
Here, blended with bourbon and jostled by
an exuberant burst of cherry, it makes a drink
that travels to a place of mystery and mixture.
Think of it like a story unfurling as you sip it;
you don't need to travel anywhere with this
drink in your hand, you've already arrived.

30ml (1oz) madeira

30ml (1oz) Luxardo maraschino liqueur

30ml (1oz) bourbon

Ice: Cubed

Garnish: Speared cherry

Equipment: Cocktail shaker, strainer

Fill a shaker with ice

Add all the ingredients

Stir gently to combine

Strain into a chilled glass

Garnish with a speared cherry

JEREZ

Sherry is the most underrated fortified wine bargain in the world, and it mixes beautifully into cocktails when its intensity is stretched out to make it even more approachable. Really good sherry is fractionally blended by experts over years in the bodegas of southern Spain, in great halls as magical and tranquil as cathedrals, with shafts of bright light breaking through their high portals picking out the occasional barrel for a preferential luminous blessing. I love the spring Feria festival in Jerez, when cool sherry fuels endless dancing. I adore the land around Jerez – fruit and vegetables seem to grow themselves, the pace of life seems as lengthened as the horizons across the plains of soil where the vineyards are. The green of the vines is one thing, but the local chalky albariza soil beneath appears almost lunar in the intense reflection of the sun's gaze. While there are many cocktails under the name 'Jerez', my version is dedicated to honouring the creativity and craft of sherry, blended with enriching orange and the power of the peach. It's a fitting tribute to Jerez, a place above all devoted to stewarding its treasures towards ever-finer flavours.

60ml (2oz) fino sherry

30ml (1oz) peach schnapps

30ml (1oz) triple sec

Ice: Cubed

Equipment: Cocktail shaker, strainer

Fill a shaker with ice

Add all the ingredients

Shake vigorously to chill

Strain into a chilled glass

You can also serve this in a rocks glass over ice if that's your preference.

ETERNAL GONG

The idea behind my Eternal Gong came from an evening scribbling notes about what flavours might unite from the world of power wines served over ice to gain unending resonance: hence the Eternal Gong. Equal parts sake, white port and fino sherry, it's all the things I love in life with wonderfully traditional flavours that have been overlooked for too long. Fino sherry brings care and craft. White port is a little-known fruity gem that's great value. Sake is technically a beer, made with rice and stacked with round umami richness. Together their varying ranges are compounded, and one sip will stay with you for longer than the imaginary gong that just sounded in your head.

30ml (1oz) sake

30ml (1oz) white port

30ml (1oz) fino sherry

Dash orange bitters

Ice: Cubed

Garnish: 3 speared frozen grapes

Equipment: Cocktail shaker, strainer, long bar spoon

Fill a shaker with ice

Add all the ingredients

Stir gently to combine

Strain into a chilled glass

Garnish with 3 speared frozen grapes

THE
SECRET BISHOP

The Secret Bishop is a venerable drink deploying an aged rum, fruity red wine and lime juice, bolstered with the red wine syrup smuggled aboard – my secret is in the mix and I'm delighted to share it with you. This cocktail was created during a serene moment of reflection, when the addition of red wine syrup brought something altogether sacred to the recipe. As you sip and share, let your refrain be the simplicity of a contented murmur of appreciation for this treat. It's a fitting recipe to praise in the temple of your heart.

60ml (2oz) seven-year-old rum

45ml (1½oz) red wine

7.5ml (¼oz) freshly squeezed lime juice

7.5ml (¼oz) red wine syrup (see page 11)

Ice: Cubed

Garnish: Lime wheel

Equipment: Cocktail shaker, strainer

Fill a shaker with ice

Add all the ingredients and shake vigorously to chill

Strain into a chilled glass

Garnish with a lime wheel

If you don't have red wine syrup, substitute with simple syrup (see page 11) to create a more classic version known as the **Bishop**.

POINSETTIA

The poinsettia is one of my mum's favourite plants. Rather like this drink, its vibrant red tone is electrifying and lights up the room. While poinsettias transform into their royal red around Christmas time, there's no reason why this drink can't brighten your days all year round. It's so simple to make, and this is an easy recipe to customise to your own taste – add a little more fizz for a lighter flourish, or a little less if it's richness you're after. Rather like a red daub in the hands of Picasso, this vivid treat can be splashed into your life and expressed in your own way.

15ml (½oz) Cointreau

30ml (1oz) cranberry juice

Champagne, to top

Garnish: Fresh cranberries

Equipment: Long bar spoon

Add the Cointreau and cranberry juice to a chilled glass

Stir to combine

Top with Champagne

Garnish with fresh cranberries

Because this drink isn't traditionally served over ice, make sure the ingredients are well chilled in advance.

SANGRIA

During many forays to Spain, Sangria has been a constant companion and I adore its colourful and creative spontaneity. I'm often asked if blending wine is considered heresy; on the contrary, I hold it as an article of faith that wine is as fit for blending as any other drink. Rioja is often the choice for Sangria. Joven or 'young' Rioja is a vibrant, fruity way to go, but any young, easy-drinking red will work a charm, rather than an iconic, aged rarity. You may be surprised by the inclusion of passion fruit juice. Think of it like the chorus you weren't expecting in the song that's top of the hit parade in the cocktail jukebox. You'd miss it if it wasn't there!

1 bottle red wine

30ml (1oz) brandy

30ml (1oz) Grand Marnier

90ml (3oz) passion fruit juice

30ml (1oz) red wine syrup (see page 11)

Soda water, to top (optional)

1 green apple, cut into 1cm (½in) cubes

1 lemon, cut into 1cm (½in) cubes

1 orange, cut into 1cm (½in) cubes

Ice: Cubed

Garnish: Rosemary sprigs

Equipment: Long bar spoon

Chop the fruit and place into a large pitcher

Add ice and all the other ingredients except the soda water

Stir gently, then leave in the fridge for at least 30 minutes before serving to let the flavours combine

Serve in chilled glasses and top with soda water if desired

Garnish with a sprig of rosemary

There are no real rules to making Sangria: have fun playing with different ingredients!

WHITE SANGRIA

Liquid brilliance. The peach wedges really make it and the flesh is so delightful to feast on once the drink is delivered. A lovely feeling of sun-blessed ease surrounds white sangria and a halo mysteriously appears around the top of your glass. For a Spanish white wine, albariño is a good bet for its fabulous freshness and gentle fragrance. If you're after a safe bet for an all-rounder, a good-value Italian white wine will always complement the vibrant fruit in this rocking recipe.

1 bottle white wine

30ml (1oz) peach schnapps

30ml (1oz) St-Germain elderflower liqueur

90ml (3oz) pink grapefruit juice

30ml (1oz) white wine syrup (see page 11)

1 peach, chopped into wedges

½ a lime, cut into wheels

Small handful chopped strawberries

Soda water, to top (optional)

Ice: Cubed

Garnish: Edible flowers

Equipment: Long bar spoon

Place all the chopped fruit in a large pitcher

Add ice and all other ingredients except the soda water

Stir gently, then leave in the fridge for at least 30 minutes before serving to let the flavours combine

Serve in chilled glasses and top with soda water if desired

Garnish with edible flowers

Once again, no rules here, have fun trying different fruit combinations.

MULLED WINE

A cracking recipe here, with maple syrup as my go-to ingredient that makes it all the more sweetly scrumptious. Of course, around the festive season and the colder months, mulled wine feels special. Take my tip – on a grey day, any time of year, or indeed to enjoy as a digestif, mulled wine can be magnificent. I'm also a big fan of serving it as an accompaniment to a favourite album, soaring symphony or favourite audiobook. It's such a contemplative drink, with heritage stretching back to the ancient Greeks who would spice up their harvest and mix wine with honey to sweeten it – a technique also favoured by the Romans. From French vin chaud to German glühwein, mulled wine is a European classic with enduring wonder and variation. You can customise it as you see fit – a fresh vanilla pod perhaps or even a slice of chilli gives it a kick.

1 bottle red wine

30ml (1oz) vodka

30ml (1oz) apricot brandy

90ml (3oz) orange juice

30ml (1oz) maple syrup

6 cloves

2 cinnamon sticks

1 star anise

1 orange, sliced

1 lemon, sliced

Equipment: Saucepan

Add all the ingredients to a saucepan

Heat gently until just simmering (do not boil)

Leave to simmer gently for 10 minutes

Serve in heatproof glasses or mugs

If you're having a party, you can keep this ticking over in a slow cooker and serve when guests are ready. It has the added benefit of infusing your home with that inimitable Christmassy aroma.

MULLED
WHITE WINE

Mulled wine is also a great mid-morning
pick-me-up. Mulled white wine enriched with
rum, Grand Marnier and spices is a cosying
drink to turn your kitchen-table gathering into
an intimate chorus. Catching up with a friend
over a warming mulled white wine feels like
sunlight from within.

1 bottle white wine

30ml (1oz) seven-year-old rum

30ml (1oz) Grand Marnier

90ml (3oz) apple juice

6 cloves

2 cinnamon sticks

¼ of a nutmeg, grated

1 orange, sliced

1 lemon, sliced

Equipment: Saucepan

Add all the ingredients to a saucepan

Heat gently until just simmering (do not boil)

Simmer for 10 minutes

Serve in seasonal glasses or mugs

Mulled cider is great to try in autumn. Swap out
the white wine for your favourite (hard) cider and
switch the rum for Calvados.

RETRO SHOOTERS

Retro shooters may be small, but they are not to be underestimated. In the main they tend toward frivolity – they're meant for high-impact moments rather than to be savoured over a long session. Enjoy their visual delights and feelgood factor!

BAKEWELL TART

Growing up I had a dear friend called James who always carried Bakewell tarts in his pockets. Although more often than not they were hot and crumbly, they were very welcome on forays and adventures for nourishment and sustenance. So this cocktail is in honour of those moments. If the day has got the better of you, knock up my Bakewell Tart and treat yourself to a little boost.

15ml (½oz) Disaronno amaretto

15ml (½oz) Baileys

15ml (½oz) Chambord

Ice: Cubed

Garnish: Spray cream and glacé cherry

Equipment: Cocktail shaker, strainer

Fill a shaker with ice

Add all the ingredients

Shake vigorously to chill

Strain into a chilled shot glass

Garnish with spray cream and a glacé cherry

B52

The satisfaction in delivering a perfect B52 is almost as delightful to me as the first time I heard the B52s singing 'Love Shack'. It's a song that divides my household. I think it's amazing; my wife Sophie is less convinced. The thing we do agree on is that layered shooters are great fun. A steady hand is required to deliver this entertainment for the eyes; it may have short stature, yet like a giant monocle it is a huge spectacle.

15ml (½oz) Kahlua

15ml (½oz) Baileys

15ml (½oz) Grand Marnier

Equipment: Long bar spoon

Pour the Kahlua into a shot glass

Hold the back of a bar spoon against the edge of the glass close to the Kahlua

Very gently pour the Baileys over the back of the spoon so it floats on top

Finish with a layer of Grand Marnier using the same pouring method

Not an easy shooter to perfect, but worth the practice. As a bonus you get to drink the versions that aren't quite right!

CHOCOLATE CAKE

My daughter makes the best chocolate cake in the world. Her title was previously held by my mother and before that my grandmother. It was only recently that my daughter surpassed all her predecessors in creating the best chocolate cake ever; when I asked how she did it, she just shrugged. I think that's what the greatest things are – a light touch, experience and enjoyment. They say if you make something with love it tastes better, and this cocktail was created as an experiential delight. I dedicate it to my daughter, the Queen of Cakes, Lily.

30ml (1oz) Frangelico

15ml (½oz) vanilla vodka

1 lemon wedge dipped in caster (superfine) sugar

Equipment: Cocktail shaker, strainer

Fill a shaker with ice

Add the Frangelico and vodka, then shake until chilled

Strain into a shot glass

Coat a wedge of lemon in caster sugar

Down the shot then bite the sugar-coated lemon wedge

If you don't have vanilla vodka, plain vodka also works.

LEMON DROP

A burst of brightness! Two of my favourite sweets of all time are the acid drop and the sherbet lemon, and this classic cocktail orbits their origins, tasting simultaneously sweet and zesty. While I wouldn't recommend carrying one of these around in a white paper bag, as the sweets used to be served in my childhood, I would certainly recommend making several Lemon Drops at once to enjoy with friends, because once one's been made, invariably more are requested – and it's a really good use of two storecupboard classics, triple sec and vodka.

30ml (1oz) vodka

15ml (½oz) triple sec

15ml (½oz) freshly squeezed lemon juice

7.5ml (¼oz) simple syrup (see page 11)

Equipment: Cocktail shaker, strainer

Fill a shaker with ice

Add all the ingredients

Shake vigorously to chill

Strain into a chilled rocks glass

SQUASHED FROG

I used to drink Squashed Frogs on cruise ships with an exuberant entertainment director called Bennie. Bennie would always lead the charge with the Squashed Frogs and where there was one Squashed Frog, there were usually several more following rapidly. I enjoyed Squashed Frogs as I watched tribute bands with Bennie – she always knew the best ones. I feel lucky to have seen 'Freddie Mercury', 'Luther Vandross' and 'Annie Lennox' through the hazy lenses of a few Squashed Frogs, floating on a distant ocean and drifting into another sunrise. Bravo, Bennie.

22.5ml (¾oz) Midori

15ml (½oz) Baileys

7.5ml (¼oz) grenadine

Equipment: Long bar spoon

Pour the Midori into a shot glass

Float the Baileys on top

Drop the grenadine on top of the drink – it will slide to the bottom of the glass, pulling some of the top layer with it

BJ

Apologies for the name of this drink but it's a classic. A retro classic, of course, traditionally enjoyed without using your hands. It's tasty, creamy and rather silly – perhaps one for the end of the night.

15ml (½oz) Kahlua

15ml (½oz) amaretto

15ml (½oz) Baileys

Garnish: Spray cream

Equipment: Long bar spoon

Pour the Kahlua into a shot glass

Hold the back of a bar spoon against the edge of the glass close to the Kahlua

Very gently pour the amaretto over the back of the spoon so it floats on top

Repeat with the Baileys so you have three clear layers

Top with spray cream

This is traditionally drunk without using your hands

MINI GUINNESS

If you want to go overboard, then 'garnish' with a full-sized pint of Guinness!

Two of my wife's favourite things are Guinness and mini things, so this is a drink for Sophie. It couldn't be more deliciously simple and of course if you want to pour a pint of Guinness on the side and sip this as a chaser, you'd be following in my wife's footsteps, whiling away the hours with pints in the enchanting County Kerry village of Ballyferriter. Sláinte.

30ml (1oz) Kahlua

15ml (½oz) Baileys

Pour the Kahlua into a shot glass

Gently pour in the Baileys so it floats on top to resemble a pint of Guinness

FLATLINER

One of my all-time favourite shooters! I hardly ever use sambuca – it seems to hide at the back of my cocktail cabinet like the memory of an exam that I don't even remember taking. Sambuca's unique anise taste is quite something, but really this is a visual treat due to the different densities of the drinks.

22.5ml (¾oz) sambuca

22.5ml (¾oz) vodka

3 or 4 drops hot sauce (e.g. Tabasco)

Make sure the vodka is well chilled before starting – ideally keep the bottle in the freezer

Pour the sambuca into a shot glass

Gently pour the chilled vodka on top so it floats

Drip the hot sauce into the vodka – it will drop down and sit perfectly between the two spirits to form a flat line

SILVER
BULLET

A classic shooter that combines the unlikely duo of Scotch and gin successfully – it has the feeling of a rich, slightly smoky Martini in miniature.

45ml (1½oz) gin

22.5ml (¾oz) Scotch whisky

Ice: Cubed

Garnish: Lemon twist

Equipment: Cocktail shaker, strainer

Fill a shaker with ice

Add all the ingredients

Shake vigorously to chill

Strain into a chilled glass

Zest the lemon twist over the drink and garnish on the side of the glass

WATERMELON SHOOTER

What's not to like about watermelon? Jolly colours, crunching flavours, exotic thrills – this is a great way to use up the mighty Midori, a scrumptious year-round cocktail to remind you that summer is never too far away.

30ml (1oz) Midori

15ml (½oz) vodka

15ml (½oz) freshly squeezed orange juice

Dash grenadine

Ice: Cubed

Equipment: Cocktail shaker, strainer

Fill a shaker with ice

Add all the ingredients

Shake vigorously to chill

Strain into a chilled glass

QUACK PEPPER

Despite not containing any Dr Pepper, the taste of my Quack Pepper reminds me of the soft drink. This is a great shooter to have in a group.

Line up the prepared collins glasses. Where each glass meets, rest a shot glass on the edge.

Knock the first shot into the glass and the rest will follow like dominoes. Everyone should then grab a drink and down it in one. A depth charge of deliciousness.

200ml (7oz) lager

60ml (2oz) cola

30ml (1oz) amaretto

Put the lager and cola in a chilled collins glass

Pour the amaretto into a shot glass

Drop the shot glass into the collins glass and quickly drink in one go

BUBBLEGUM

Bubblegum is one of the weirdest flavours in the world. I love it, even though I don't love the way bubblegum gets stuck on pavements, the back of trousers, on a sock or even in hair. However, all of that can be avoided by creating this cocktail, which is also known as Liquid Bubblegum – and you don't even have to chew it.

15ml (½oz) crème de banane

15ml (½oz) Baileys

15ml (½oz) blue curaçao

Ice: Cubed

Equipment: Cocktail shaker, strainer, long bar spoon

Fill a shaker with ice

Add all the ingredients

Shake vigorously to chill

Strain into a chilled shot glass

Aka **Bazooka Joe** or **Liquid Bubblegum**.

SPRINGBOK

My favourite area of South Africa is the Swartland. I love the boutique wine estates there, and the characterful, youthful, reinvigorating enterprise of the growers who have become owners over the years. With its colours of the Springboks national rugby team, this is the drink I raise to them.

30ml (1oz) green crème de menthe

15ml (½oz) Amarula cream liqueur (or Baileys if you don't have Amarula)

Pour the crème de menthe into a shot glass

Gently top with Amarula so it floats on the surface

BIRTHDAY CAKE

I love sprinkles on my birthday cake, but with a drink this tasty, I wish it was my birthday every single day of the year – and I couldn't imagine a more delicious present to give to you. No need to unwrap it – consider this a gift card: 'Dear you, cheers. Lots of love from me.' Happy sipping and here's to a cracking cocktail!

30ml (1oz) Baileys

30ml (1oz) white crème de cacao

Ice: Cubed

Garnish: Grenadine and cake sprinkles

Equipment: Cocktail shaker, strainer

Dip the rim of a chilled shot glass into grenadine then dip into cake sprinkles to form a rim

Fill a shaker with ice and add all the ingredients

Shake vigorously to chill

Strain into the sprinkle-rimmed shot glass

If you have an iced birthday cake to hand, instead of using grenadine you can dip the rim of the glass in icing first before adding the sprinkles.

FIRECREAM

An old-school classic with a new name: easy, fun and something sweet. Since it looks a little scary, it's best served if you're feeling daring. Or on Halloween!

30ml (1oz) peach schnapps

15ml (½oz) Baileys

7.5ml (¼oz) grenadine

Pour the peach schnapps into a shot glass

Gently pour the Baileys over the schnapps so it forms a layer

Drop the grenadine on top of the shooter. It will fall to the bottom of the glass, pulling some of the top layer with it

INDEX

ACKNOWLEDGEMENTS

First and foremost my heartfelt gratitude and thanks to Sarah Lavelle at Quadrille for the inception and inspiration for this book. It has been such fun to work on and I really couldn't imagine anyone more kind, steady and dedicated to work with.

My heart beats with deep delight for Seb Munsch, my wingman behind the bar – cheers buddy, you rock.

My literary agent, Gordon Wise – you are a boundless realm of brilliance.

Thank you to Claire Rochford, Alicia House, Emma Marijewycz, Laura Willis, Euan Ferguson, Laura Eldridge and Nik Ginelli at Quadrille and Hardie Grant for all the magnificent support bringing the book into the world.

To my amazing team who brought the cocktails to life through the lens, Matt Russell (best playlists in the business), Loïc Parisot, Max Robinson and all the crew on Turnpike Lane who made those moments so magical.

My assistant Ellie James, who is without question the greatest plate spinner of all time, my wife Sophie for bravely tasting some of my weirder concoctions whilst encouraging me to wade ever deeper into the wonderful world of cocktails.

I'd also like to raise my glass to Graham Holter who gave me my first ever job writing about drinks and to everyone who's served me a cocktail from behind a bar – I had a great time, so cheers.

Most of all, I'm grateful to you for picking up this book, thank you – and may it bring you joy!